The Story of Mohammed
Islam Unveiled

Harry Richardson

This book is dedicated to all the people of the world, whatever their beliefs may be.

Acknowledgement

In writing this book, I had the privilege of standing on the shoulders of Bill Warner of the Centre for the Study of Political Islam. Bill is not just an intellectual giant but a true gentleman. I would therefore like to express my gratitude to him, I could not have written this book without his pioneering work.

Contents

Introduction

Why would a non-Muslim want to read the story of Mohammed? For many Westerners, the life of a self-proclaimed Prophet[1], who died more than 1300 years ago in a remote part of the world, might sound not only dull, but also completely irrelevant. In fact it is neither. During his life Mohammed created a religious and political movement called Islam. A quarter of the world's population is now Islamic and it is the world's fastest growing religion by far. Importantly, the influence of this religion currently stretches into more aspects of our societies than most of us realize.

After studying Islamic doctrine and history, it soon became clear that the majority of what we hear about Islam's goals and its influence on the actions and beliefs of Muslims, is entirely wrong. This lack of understanding has been the root cause of horrendous policy failures in areas such as the "War on terror," Middle Eastern foreign policy, the Arab- Israeli conflict etc. which tend to dominate our daily news cycle.

It is also clear that the reason for these failures is widespread ignorance of the doctrine of Islam throughout all sections of Western society. This includes politicians, academics, journalists, teachers, right on down to the man in the street. Given the rapidly rising threats from Islamic "extremists" and the growing number of conflicts involving Muslims, this would seem to be a failure of epic proportions.

It is for this reason that I have written this book. I wanted it to be widely read and so made it as simple and entertaining as possible. It is reasonably short and avoids dry theological discussion. If you have an interest in what lies behind the news stories we see every day, you should find it both interesting and relevant.

By the end, you should also have a good grasp of the doctrine of Islam. You will know what this doctrine expects of Muslims and how it affects the societies in which Muslims are living. Most importantly, this knowledge will give you a whole new understanding of issues involving Islam. Conflicts around the globe, terrorism, immigration,

---

[1] Mohammed insisted that he was the final Prophet of Allah (God). People who believe him are called Muslims. People who don't are called non-Muslims (the Arabic word is "Kaffir").

treatment of women etc. can never be properly understood without a basic grasp of Islamic doctrine.

Islamic scholars have always known that the key to understanding Islam is the story of Mohammed's life. This is good news, because Mohammed was an extremely interesting character.

Unlike any other prophet, Mohammed was also a political and military leader. He insisted that Muslims should fight when called upon to put Islam in control of the whole world. During the last nine years of his life, he and his followers were involved in acts of violent conquest on average once every seven weeks. By the time he died, he was the King of all Arabia with not a single enemy left standing. The key to his success was a new system of warfare called Jihad which Westerners usually translate as "Holy War," but which is in fact far more than this.

More is known about Mohammed than any other religious leader[2]. Strangely however, even in the Islamic world, few people know his story. This is not an accident. The life of Mohammed is the perfect example for all Muslims to follow. As such, it is the basis for the Islamic religion itself. You would expect then, that Muslims would be as familiar with Mohammed as Christians are with Jesus. This is not the case however.

Young Muslims are taught to recite the Koran in Arabic but are sternly dissuaded from understanding its meaning. Four fifths of Muslims do not even speak modern Arabic, let alone the archaic form the Koran is written in. Generally speaking, only those Muslims who are committed enough to want to become Islamic Religious leaders or "Imams" learn about Mohammed's life. The rest are expected to follow directions from these leaders who keep this knowledge to themselves.

Today, Muslim populations are exploding across the world as Western birth rates plummet. More than ninety percent of all wars and armed conflicts today involve Muslims. The great majority of terror attacks (more than twenty thousand just in the nine years since 9/11[3]) are also carried out by Muslim Jihadists. The largest and most influential block of countries in the UN (despite their current lack of veto powers) are the fifty seven members of the Organization of Islamic Cooperation.

---

[2] Centre for the Study of Political Islam

[3] http://thereligionofpeace.com

These nations also control the lion's share of the planet's dwindling oil reserves.

In years to come these trends will almost certainly accelerate. This will give Islam increasing power, not just in the lives of Muslims, but also in the lives of non-Muslims. Unbelievers will increasingly find themselves constricted by laws and demands which reflect this growing influence. This expanding Islamic power and influence is going to affect you, your children and your grandchildren. If you want to know, "how" and "why" then this book is the quickest and easiest way to find out. For those seeking a more serious understanding of this complex subject, this book is an excellent first step. It will set you in the right direction and serve as a solid foundation.

Tony Blair, George Bush and most other world leaders, academics, journalists and opinion formers in the Western world insist that Islam is a religion of peace which has a few violent radicals, angry at Western foreign policy.

Ayatollah Khomeini devoted his entire life to the study of Islamic doctrine. He became the spiritual and religious leader of the Islamic Republic of Iran and the foremost religious authority for the entire Shiite world (differences between Shia and Sunni Islam are fairly superficial). Here is what he had to say about Islam and warfare.

"But those who study Islamic Holy War will understand why Islam wants to conquer the whole world. Those who know nothing of Islam pretend that Islam counsels against war. Those (who say this) are witless."

Read the story of Mohammed for yourself and see if you can figure out who is right.

1 Early Life

(If you think this book has been written to promote a sinister agenda or somehow encourage harm to Muslims, then please go to the end and read the appendix first.)

Mohammed ibn Abdullah (The Prophet Mohammed) was born in 570AD, in a town called Mecca in what is now called Saudi Arabia. At that time Arabia was not a country, it was an area inhabited by a collection of tribes. It was and remains, a hot, dry and inhospitable landscape where people survived herding sheep and goats. Some dates were also cultivated in the North. Blood feuds were not uncommon. These would generally be resolved through the principle of an eye for an eye, a tooth for a tooth. Sometimes blood money would be paid to resolve a killing.

Mecca was a holy town and a centre for all different kinds of religions. There was (and still is) a building named the Kabah which held a sacred stone. This is believed to have been a meteorite. There was also a well, whose water was thought to be holy and to have medicinal powers. Tribes from all around Arabia would come to Mecca to worship their various deities. There were even a few Christians and Jews living there; it was very multicultural. Mohammed came from the nobility of Mecca who were known as the Quraysh and his clan was known as the Hashim. The main God of the Quraysh was Allah who is believed by many to be the Moon God, (which would explain why every Mosque has a crescent moon on top). Many other Gods were also worshipped. Because it was a holy place, fighting was not allowed in Mecca. Violent disputes had to be settled outside of the town.

Mohammed's father died before he was born and his mother died when he was five. He was then raised by his grandfather, until he too

1

died. His uncle, Abu Talib then took over his care. Abu Talib was a powerful member of the Quraysh. He seems to have been a kindly figure who, while he was alive, protected Mohammed and treated him well.

The main business of the Quraysh was religion, though they also made money from trading. When he grew up Mohammed was hired by a wealthy widow named Khadija. She ran a business trading with Syria. Mohammed managed the caravans and did the deals with the Syrians. Syria was a Christian country at that time and far more sophisticated and cosmopolitan than Arabia. At that time it was in fact, more sophisticated and cosmopolitan than most of Europe. The Arabs took their alphabet from the Syrian Christians. Writing was however, restricted to business transactions only. There were no books written in Arabic at that time. Religious traditions were passed down by word-of-mouth. Christians and Jews were known as the people of the book because they possessed written Scriptures. Mohammed did well as a trader and made a good profit for Khadija. After a while Khadija proposed marriage to him. They had four daughters and two sons together[4].

Because of his background, Mohammed was familiar with many different religions. He was of course very familiar with the rituals of his own clan, the pagan Arabs of Mecca. Many of these pagan rituals would be incorporated into Islam. There were also some Jews in Mecca and his wife's cousin was a Christian. Since most religions were not written down, it was not uncommon for people to have different versions of each religion, or even to start their own type of worship.

Important Facts:
To be a Muslim means to accept that Mohammed was the perfect Human Being. His life is the example for all Muslims to follow in every way possible. Of course not all Muslims are very successful in this endeavour but the level of devoutness of a Muslim is judged by how closely he follows Mohammed's example and teachings. This fact is not disputed in Islam. That is why it is so important to know his story. There is even a word to describe Mohammed's behaviour, which is "Sunnah"

---

[4] Only one of his daughters, Fatima survived to adulthood.

Note:

Some people may feel that this book should not be read for moral reasons. Before I go any further I would therefore like to make something very clear. I am a huge fan of religious freedom. People should be allowed to believe what they want and worship in any way they see fit. If a group of Christians wants to worship in a weird or unusual way it doesn't bother me one bit.

If, however those people form a political organization and start trying to influence the way their society is run then I will likely take an interest. If I don't agree with their political agenda or methods, I assert my right to criticize these activities. This is not a religious criticism; it is a political criticism.

This book is not overly concerned with religious aspects of Islam. We will not be investigating its religious beliefs or practices too deeply. What I will be commenting on are the political objectives, political agenda and political methods of Islam. These are clearly laid down in Islamic Doctrine. How Muslims interact with each other or interact with their chosen Deity is a religious matter. That doesn't interest me at all. How they interact with non-Muslims, (who they refer to as Kaffirs) is a political matter and does concern me. As this story unfolds you will soon see why.

Bibliography

The original source of most of this material is Ibn Ishaq's book, *Sirat Rasul Allah* (The Story of the Prophet of Allah) or just *The Sira.* Ibn Ishaq is the most revered and trusted Muslim scholar of all time. This work was compiled around 100 years after Mohammed's death which makes it his oldest surviving biography. It is the absolute definitive biographical account of Mohammed's life for Islamic scholars.

It was translated into English in 1955 by Professor of Arabic, Alfred Guillaume, under the title *The Life of Muhammad* with the help of a number of Arab professors. This is still the most widely used English translation for both Muslims and non-Muslims.

This direct translation has been superbly simplified and rearranged, by Bill Warner of the Centre for the Study of Political Islam. He has included material from other well trusted sources. This gives clarity and context to a story which previously took enormous amounts of painstaking study to understand. The title of his book is *Mohammed and the Unbelievers.* Most of the quotes used will come from this book (which is referenced back to *The Sira* by a system of margin numbers contained in the original text).

3

2 Islam is Founded

When he was around Forty years old, Mohammed started to take month-long retreats, to pray and to perform the religious practices of the Quraysh. He began to have visions where he was visited by the Angel Gabriel. He said that Gabriel would teach him scriptures. Gabriel then told him to recite these scriptures so he could teach them to his followers. These would later be written down by his followers and were compiled after his death into what is known today as the Koran. His wife Khadija supported him and became the first convert to the new religion of Islam. In Arabic Islam means "submission". Khadija was soon joined by Mohammed's adopted son and other family members. Eventually some other people outside of the family joined them too. As Mohammed gained followers he became more confident. Soon he began to preach quite openly from his new religion.

In the beginning this did not cause a problem. The Quraysh were very tolerant of different religions as that was how they made their money. For them, more religion meant more money. If Mohammed's new religion brought in more people to worship, it would be all the better.

Things soon began to sour however, as the tone of Mohammed's teachings became steadily less tolerant. Mohammed began to teach that his religion was the right one (which was okay) but that all the other religions were false (which was not). He mocked the other religions and ridiculed their Gods. What was even worse for the Quraysh, was Mohammed's claim that because their ancestors were not Muslims, they were burning in hell. For the Quraysh whose ancestors were sacred, this was intolerable. They begged him to stop doing this and return to promoting his own religion without rubbishing theirs.

4

When he refused, the Quraysh wanted to kill him. Unfortunately for them, Mohammed still enjoyed the protection of his powerful uncle, Abu Talib. The Quraysh tried to offer his uncle inducements. They wanted him to hand over Mohammed so that they could kill him, but he steadfastly refused.

Mohammed was clearly a charismatic preacher who gradually gained more followers. This increased the divisions within the community. There were quarrels and constant bickering. Mecca was a small town and everybody knew each other's business.

What had once been a peaceful and profitable community was now split badly, between the Quraysh and the new converts who were known as Muslims (which means those who have submitted).

Some of the less powerful Muslims and especially slaves who had converted, were treated quite badly by the Quraysh. Fortunately for them, Mohammed's uncle was able to protect them all from serious harm. Some of the Meccans who converted were also among the strongest and most powerful members of the community. It gradually became harder for the Quraysh to do anything about Mohammed. Although he had called them stupid, insulted their gods and claimed that their ancestors were burning in hell, they were unable to stop him.

The Quraysh tried to reason with Mohammed and even tried to cut him a deal. They offered him money, or even the leadership of the tribe, if he would just stop his preaching. Mohammed refused, insisting that he was only the messenger of Allah and had no choice in the matter.

Author's Comments:

Before I get too far into Islam, I want to give a very brief overview of Christianity. Like it or not, if you grew up in a "Western" country then your ethics, your sense of right and wrong, are based upon Christian teachings, as are the laws which our society makes.

People who grow up in different cultures may have a different definition of what is right and wrong. To give an example, what a Viking might have considered to be "the right thing to do," would probably be seen as seriously anti-social in modern day Denmark.

Islam has a set of ethics. In order to explain these ethics I will sometimes be comparing them to Christian ethics. This is not because I'm promoting Christianity but because most Westerners,

5

(including myself) understand it far better than for instance Hinduism or Buddhism.

The basis of Christian (and Jewish) ethics is the Ten Commandments which we are all probably familiar with. Don't steal, cheat, lie, kill, covet etc. These are then capped off with the Golden Rule which is:

"Do unto others as you would have them do unto you."

From the Golden Rule are derived the other principles of freedom of speech, the rule of law, equality, tolerance etc. which underpin the laws and customs of most Western countries. Growing up in a society based on this Golden Rule, we tend to believe that it is universal and not even remotely a radical idea. Keep in mind however, that the man who popularized this idea 2000 years ago, got nailed to a tree for it.

Despite this, the idea gained currency and continued to spread. By the time of Mohammed's birth, Christianity was the dominant religion throughout most of the Middle East, North Africa and Europe.

The Golden Rule and the Ten Commandments however, ARE NOT the basis for every religion and society. As you will soon find out they are definitely not the basis of Islam.

Islam is difficult to explain clearly. In some ways, it is a bit like a giant jigsaw puzzle. I could show you a single piece of a jigsaw and tell you for instance, that it is a tiger's nose. Although it might not look like a tiger's nose, it is not until you see it surrounded by the other pieces that you can tell what it really is. Some of the things I write may seem strange, or even ridiculous to someone who has grown up in a Western country with Christian based ethics. Hopefully however, by the time you finish this book you will be able to see each piece in the context of the whole picture.

3 Islam Grows

Mohammed stayed in Mecca for thirteen years after declaring himself a prophet. The first half of the Koran was written during this time and is known as the Koran of Mecca. The revelations in the Meccan Koran tell repeatedly that Mohammed is the Messenger of God and that all those who disbelieve him will burn in hell. There are also stories of people from the past who rejected their prophets. These people were consequently destroyed and are now burning in hell.

According to Mohammed, many of the biblical characters such as Abraham, Moses and even Jesus (who he claimed was not the Son of God but a prophet) were Muslims. No mention of the Islamic religion has ever been found which pre-dates Mohammed however. He further claimed that he was the last in the line of these prophets and that the Koran was God's final message.

The Koran takes a number of stories from the Bible and retells them quite differently, in order to make a different point. In this retelling, the message is always about how the Jews ignored their prophets and were then punished by God.

This is the religious part of the Koran, which contains the biblical stories and religious themes. Mohammed used these basic themes quite skilfully to answer most of the questions his critics put to him.

Mohammed was obviously quite charismatic and very self-confident. He also had the ability to package his message in a quite beautifully poetic form. The first half of the Koran is written poetically, which also makes it easier to memorize. Consequently he attracted quite a number of followers and as his power grew, so did his desire for it. He was extremely narcissistic and seemed to

7

care only for the adoration of others. The fact that he tore apart his home town and even his own family did not seem to bother him.

When his uncle lay dying he went to his bedside and asked him to accept Islam. His uncle muttered something and then died. Mohammed's companion said that he thought his uncle had accepted Islam. Mohammed did not hear him clearly however and declared therefore that his uncle would burn in hell. Abu Talib had raised him from being a child. He then secured him his first job which led to his successful marriage. Later, he protected Mohammed from all the trouble which he had created himself. Because he had refused to submit to Islam however, Mohammed declared that he was burning in hell.

That year his wife Khadija also died. He married a widow named Sauda and was betrothed to a six-year-old girl named Aisha who was the daughter of his most ardent follower.

Important facts:

Muslims obviously believe that Mohammed was the final Prophet of Allah. From a non-Muslim viewpoint however, he was simply a genius who designed and defined Islam for a singular purpose; to make the whole world worship him (or to worship Allah through him which is pretty much the same thing).

To do this, he made sure that Islam could never be changed. Mohammed insisted that to be a Muslim, a person must declare that there is no God but Allah and Mohammed is his prophet (there are four other "pillars" of Islam but this is the most important by far). This is the definition of what it means to be a Muslim. Mohammed also declared himself to be the last prophet of Islam. In doing so, he cleverly prevented anyone from hijacking his religion down the track.

Despite claiming to be the last in the line of Jewish prophets he also ensured that the Jews could have no claim on his religion. Mohammed insisted that the Jews (and Christians) had falsified their Bible. He said that this was to hide the fact that he had been prophesied in the real Bible (there is no evidence to support this claim). He also forbade Muslims from reading the Bible or the Torah (Jewish Bible). Muslims therefore can only read about Biblical prophets such as Abraham or Moses through Mohammed's retelling. This is often quite different, sometimes illogically so, from the original Bible stories.

The point to all this is that Mohammed is not just a central figure in Islam, Mohammed IS Islam. In Churchill's day, Muslims were referred to as Mohammedans, (people who follow Mohammed) which is a fairly accurate description. To be a Muslim is to believe that Mohammed is the perfect man and that the Koran, as revealed to Mohammed only, is the perfect (and only) word of Allah. A true Muslim therefore follows the words of Allah (as found in the Koran) and the example, or traditions of Mohammed (which are recorded in his biographies).

This clever design of Islam means that it can never be changed. The Koran can't be changed because it is the perfect word of Allah. Mohammed's life can't be changed because he's dead.

Muslims are incredibly serious about how perfect the Koran is. To give an example of this, several chapters of the Koran start with three Arabic letters. No one knows what this means but they will never be removed because the Koran is perfect and unalterable.

To summarize then; Islam is Mohammed, Islam has never changed, Islam will never change. To change Islam, you would have to take Mohammed out of it and then it wouldn't be Islam any more. As Barry Sheene so eloquently put it,

"If my uncle was a woman he'd be my [word deleted] Aunty." It is a logical absurdity. Christianity changed and evolved because it is based on broad principles, such as the golden rule, which can be debated and interpreted. There isn't much to debate with Mohammed, he either did something or he didn't. People who think that Islam should, or even could change are therefore likely to be disappointed.

4 Emigration to Medina

Once a year, people from all over Arabia came to Mecca for a religious fair. Many of them began to hear of Mohammed and wished to hear him preach. In this way he gained new followers from outside of Mecca. One group came from Medina, which is a town to the North of Mecca.

Medina contained five tribes, three were Jewish and two Arab. The Jewish tribes were generally better educated and wealthier. There were quarrels between the Arab tribes and also between Arabs and Jews. This had spilled over into bloodshed.

Some of the Medinan Arabs who had converted to Islam invited Mohammed and his followers to come to Medina. They thought that he might be a unifying influence who would bring peace to their tribes.

The next year when the annual fair came around again, Mohammed took the Medinans to a hillside outside of Mecca, called Aquaba. There he had them swear an oath to him, which became known as the Oath of Aquaba. This oath included a promise to fight to the death in the service of Mohammed. In return for this, he promised them paradise. This was the first time that Mohammed's teachings included the threat of killing; it is also the beginning of the Islamic calendar.

The Quraysh soon heard about this and hatched a plot to kill Mohammed. They figured that if they did not take action now, he would return from Medina with an army and make war on them. Mohammed's followers had mostly left for Medina already and his uncle had died. Now he had no one to protect him. Mohammed heard of the plot and fled Mecca. He hid in a cave for three days until the heat had died down and then continued on the 10-day trip to Medina.

Author's Comments:

At this point in time Mohammed had been a prophet for 13 years. He was slightly more than half way through his career as a religious leader. He had acquired around 150 followers, the majority of whom were poor and uneducated and had made many powerful enemies. Mohammed had made many threats to his enemies, (i.e. anyone who would not accept that he was God's only prophet) about punishments in the afterlife. His teachings however, were essentially of a religious nature. In other words, they were about how Muslims should interact with Allah, or with other Muslims. They were not however, political in nature (how Muslims should interact with non-Muslims). Islam has a habit of dividing things in two. The Koran is no exception and is divided into two separate halves. There is the Koran of Mecca, which is mostly religious and the Koran of Medina, which is essentially political in nature.

In the last chapter I laboured the point that Muslims are obliged to follow Mohammed's teaching and traditions. I would like to add some important caveats here, because you may soon be thinking something like "I know a Muslim who doesn't do that" or "how come most Muslims don't do that."

1) Not all Muslims follow their religion devoutly any more than followers of any other religion. Some are very devout but many are not. A Muslim may behave in a way which is against the teaching of Islam such as drinking alcohol. This doesn't mean that Islam permits drinking alcohol. It just means that not everyone follows the rules all the time. Islam can affect Muslims but Muslims cannot affect Islam.

2) Muslims are supposed to follow the example of Mohammed. There are however, a number of different ways in which Mohammed behaved in order to achieve his aims. These methods depended largely on the circumstances. If I wanted to be kind I would describe him as "opportunistic." I'll be explaining this in more detail down the track as it is important. Whilst many Muslims do not follow Mohammed's more unpleasant methods, most of them seem to share his goals.

3) Muslims in general are very ignorant of the details of their religion, this is not an accident. Most Muslims don't speak Arabic and yet their books are written in an archaic form of it. Islamic scholars insist however, that these books cannot be translated. This is just one reason why, until recently, it was incredibly difficult to understand these books, (or even to know which books were important) unless you were taught by Islamic scholars.

5 Sharia Law and the Koran of Medina

Right from the start, things were different in Medina. Mohammed already had a number of followers there. Once his followers from Mecca joined him, he had a sizeable group. Included in these were some of Mecca's fiercest warriors. Importantly, unlike the Meccans, the clans of Medina were already deeply divided amongst themselves. Because the Muslims were prepared to stick together, Mohammed became the most powerful man in Medina. The Medinan clans also gave him the power to mediate disputes believing that he would be a good, neutral arbitrator.

Mohammed soon set about consolidating this power. He built a Mosque and a compound nearby for himself, his followers and his growing number of wives. He wrote a charter which was to be the basis for the law of Medina. This law was based on two different sets of rules. One set of rules would apply to the Muslims and a different set of rules would apply to the Kaffirs (non-Muslims). These rules became known as Sharia Law.

Mohammed divided the world into the Muslims, who believed in him and the Kaffirs, who did not. Now this division was set down in law and became the basis of the Islamic religion.

All Muslims were henceforth to be members of a nation known as the Ummah. They were bound to help all other Muslims, especially in conflicts with Kaffirs.

A Muslim should not kill another Muslim, nor help a Kaffir against a Muslim. Muslims were sworn to avenge violence against other Muslims but Kaffirs should never fight against Muslims. Jews who were allied with the Muslims were to be treated fairly. If they went to war with the Muslims they would help pay for the war. They were also obliged to come to the aid of Muslims who were attacked. Mohammed was to be the final judge of all disputes and disagreements. The world was now divided into two halves. Dar al Islam (the land of Islam) which would be ruled by Sharia Law and Dar al Harb (the land of war) which was the rest of the planet. This division is still a key component of Islam today.

This new legal code turned non-Muslims into distinctly second-class citizens. Many of the Arabs converted to Islam to avoid this discrimination and because of pressure applied to them. They did not truly believe however. Mohammed referred to these pretend Muslims as "hypocrites". Mohammed was now so powerful in Medina that no Arab would openly criticize him.

Author's Comments:

From here on in this story becomes much more shocking. For the sake of authenticity I will be quoting frequently from Islam's Holy Books. Before I start doing this however I would like to give a better understanding of how they work and how they fit together.

These books can be considered as a Trilogy, consisting of *The Sira*, (*Sirat Rasul Allah* by Ibn Ishaq) the *hadith* and *The Koran*. *The Sira* makes up the bulk of what you are reading. It is a straightforward biography and needs little explanation. If a quote comes from *The Sira*, it will be preceded by the letter I and then a number. This relates to margin numbers in the original text.

A hadith is a short story or "tradition". These are usually about a paragraph long. They are usually related by a companion of Mohammed, about something he did or said. Confusingly, a collection of hadith is called…. a hadith. These stories come to us via a number of re-tellings, a little like Chinese whispers. Many of the compilers were not rigorous in verifying these stories. They produced compilations of hadith which are considered unreliable or "weak".

There are two collections of hadith which are considered to stand head and shoulders above the others. These are the hadith of Al-Bukhari and of Abu Al-Husayn Muslim. These two collections are often referred to as "sahih" (e.g. sahih Bukhari) which in Arabic means "authentic". Any quotes I use will come from these two "canonical" hadith although there are four others which are considered "reliable".

Islamic scholars often trawl through the collections of weaker hadith. They search for extra information about Mohammed's life which is not included in the stronger and better known hadith. However, anything which contradicts Bukhari or Muslim would not be considered to be correct. The idea that "greater" Jihad means "to struggle to improve oneself" comes from a weak collection of hadith[5].

The Koran

In one sense the Koran is the most important of the three sets of books. It makes up only around 18% of Islamic doctrine and rather less if you take out the mountain of repetition it contains. Importantly however, it is considered to be the verbatim word of God, his last message to his faithful followers and utterly perfect in every way.

To give yet another example of how seriously Muslims take this, Persian rug makers who produce incredibly beautiful and intricate silk and wool rugs, always put a tiny fault in each one, (although you or I would almost certainly never find it). This is because they believe that only the Koran is perfect and therefore nothing else should be.

To reinforce this incredible importance, I will be highlighting any quotes which come from the Koran.

The Koran is not like the Bible which can be easily understood simply by reading it. Firstly, it is not written in chronological order. The surahs (chapters) are arranged by length from longest to shortest (except for the first). This is believed to make it easier to memorize.

On its own, this would probably be confusing enough. To make things even more confusing however, earlier verses are cancelled out, or "abrogated" by later ones.

The Koran was claimed by Mohammed, to be the verbatim Word of God. It soon became clear to people however, that different parts of the Koran contradicted each other. When questioned about this, Allah sent down a new verse:

2:106 Whatever of Our revelations we repeal or cause to be forgotten, we will replace with something superior or comparable. Do you not know that Allah has power over all things? Do you not know that Allah reigns sovereign over the heavens and earth and besides him you have no protector or helper?

---

[5] Abu Fadl, 'Greater and "Lesser" Jihad'

In fact, as many as 225 verses of the Koran are abrogated (cancelled) by later verses.

The Koran is not written in chronological order. Since later verses cancel earlier ones, it is therefore impossible to understand its meaning without knowing the order in which it was written. To do this it must be read in conjunction with the other Islamic sacred texts, *The Sira* and the hadith.

There is another barrier to understanding the Koran. Muslim scholars insist that its meaning cannot be translated into another language. This claim is of course ridiculous. The Koran has been translated many times and all these translations give quite similar meanings. The Koran is written in poetic form which makes it easier to memorise. When translated into another language the poetry is lost, but the meaning remains.

Only a minority of Muslims speak Arabic. Very few of those who do would clearly understand the ancient, thirteen hundred year old Arabic of the Koran. This makes a study of the Koran difficult, even for Muslims. For Kaffirs, (non-Muslims) it is even harder. Until recently, *The Koran* and other Islamic holy books, had never been arranged to give a clear and concise meaning. This made it impossible for a layman to understand them.

It may be tempting to dismiss these facts as the quirks of a religion which is still fundamentally similar to our own. It is also true that the Catholic Church once refused to allow the Bible to be translated out of ancient Latin. However, once we manage to get past these barriers and find the real message of Islam, the reason soon becomes clear.

Mohammed claimed that the Koran was God's final word. He insisted that it contains everything anyone would ever need to know. It is however, quite limited in its scope. It is the most revered of the Islamic holy books. In terms of *understanding* Islam however, it is actually the least important. In fact, of the much vaunted "five pillars of Islam," there is not enough information in the Koran to perform even one of these "pillars". What the Koran does tell us repeatedly however, is that to be a true Muslim you must follow the example of Mohamed which is contained in *The Sira* and the hadith (the "Sunnah" of Mohammed).

6 The Jews Fall from Grace

The few Jews who lived in Mecca were not very knowledgeable about their religion. When Mohammed claimed to be a Jewish Prophet, they took his word for it. In Medina there were many Jews. Among these were rabbis and experts on the Jewish religion. As a consequence, Mohammed faced some serious questioning about his beliefs and was unable to convince the Jews that he was one of their Prophets. They could clearly see that the Koran did not tally with their Scriptures.

This infuriated Mohammed who began disparaging the Jews, claiming that they had falsified their Scriptures. He said they had taken out the part which prophesied his coming. In actual fact, Allah of the Koran is fundamentally different from the God of the Torah, (the Jewish Bible or "Old Testament").

For example, the God of the Bible/Torah is said to love all people. He even loves those who sin and refuse to believe in him. Mohammed's God Allah however, despises the unbelievers (Kaffirs).

Mohammed also made the same accusation about Christians falsifying the Bible; yet copies of the Bible and of the Jewish Torah have been found which predate Mohammed by hundreds, or sometimes even thousands of years. These are the same books as those we have today.

Hatred of Jews was to colour the religion of Islam from this point on. In fact, Mohammed's biography contains more hatred of Jews than Hitler's Mein Kampf[6]. Until this point, Mohammed had told his followers to pray towards Jerusalem. Now he changed his mind and told them to pray towards the Kabah in Mecca. He began to speak badly of both Jews and Christians. The Koran claimed that Allah would turn them into pigs and apes.

---

[6] Centre for the Study of Political Islam statistical analysis of Islamic Holy Texts

Child Brides

Not long after his arrival in Medina, Mohammed consummated his marriage to Aisha who was now nine years old. Mohammed reluctantly agreed for her to bring her dolls into the harem. This was a difficult decision for him as he hated images of any kind. This included any kind of sculptures or paintings. Aisha's age at this time is verified by a number of the most reliable Hadith. There are a few weaker Hadith which would seem to contradict this fact. These are sometimes quoted by Muslims who wish to deny the charge that Mohammed was a paedophile. Bear in mind however that the most revered manual of Sharia Law, (which is based on the example of Mohammed's life) gives instructions for divorcing a wife who has not yet reached puberty[7].

From Bukhari's Hadith:

B5,58,234 Mohammed engaged me when I [Aisha] was a girl of six years. We went to Medina; then I got ill and my hair fell down. Later on my hair grew again and my mother, Um Ruman, came to me while I was playing in a swing with some of my girl friends. She called me and I went to her, not knowing what she wanted to do to me. She caught me by the hand and made me stand at the door of the house. I was breathless then and when my breathing became all right, she took some water and rubbed my face and head with it.
Then she took me into the house. There in the house I saw some Helper women who said, "Best wishes and Allah's Blessing and good luck." Then she entrusted me to them and they prepared me for the marriage. Unexpectedly Mohammed came to me in the forenoon and my mother handed me over to him. At that time I was a girl of nine years of age.

Author's Comments:

Fecundism: (word derived from fecundity) is the politics of wilfully promoting high birth rate among a group for the sake of enlarging its numbers related to other groups and consequently, its political influence[8].

---

[7] Reliance of the Traveller translated by Nuh Ha Mim Keller, by Amana Publications, 1994.
[8] Wikipedia

It is of course tempting to make a moral judgment about the rights and wrongs of this situation. By today's (Western) standards, what Mohammed did was both morally repugnant and highly illegal. Many societies have had lower ages of consent than we have today however. Nine years old would seem to be at the bottom end of the scale. In 7th century Arabia however, this act didn't seem to cause much controversy. It would seem therefore, to be within the norms of Mohammed's society. I also feel compelled to point out that any number of self-declared holy men have used their position to procure sex with young girls. If this was the worst thing that Mohammed had done, I probably wouldn't be writing this now.

As we will soon see however, from the time he declared himself to be a prophet, Mohammed seemed to have just one overriding aim. He seems to have been determined that the whole world would accept him as the final Prophet of God. Every aspect of his life and his religion became focused on this one goal. Mohammed's large sexual appetite is plainly documented in Islam's Holy Books. To understand his attitude to women and sex however, they need to be viewed in the context of political and military expansion. This may seem like idle speculation at this stage. As this story unfolds, other pieces of the jigsaw will soon fall into place which will make this abundantly clear.

Mohammed wasn't the first to use Fecundism and he certainly wasn't the last. The Catholic Church is one of the more famous examples. Chairman Mao used it to great effect. The subsequent Chinese leadership had to implement the "One Child" policy however, to prevent the negative consequences of overpopulation, such as hunger, poverty and overcrowding.

Islam doesn't care about these consequences. They are in fact the hallmarks of most Islamic societies.

Overcrowding leads to Muslims emigrating whenever possible, to set up in new territories. The process then begins all over again. This has been part of Islam's strategy since Mohammed's "Hijra," or emigration to Medina. Before I outline the ways in which Islam achieves this high birth rate, let's have a look at what Islam has to say about a woman's place in society[9].

The best way to learn about Sharia Law is to examine the actual laws. The best source is Reliance of the Traveller, translated by Nuh Ha Mim Keller, by Amana Publications, 1994. The Sharia is

---

[9] Bill Warner of the Centre for the Study of Political Islam.

organized in an outline form and each case quoted below will be referenced by the index number.

Forced marriage
A woman may be forced to marry a person whom she does not want.

M3.13 Whenever the bride is a virgin, the father or the father's father may marry her without her permission, though it is recommended to ask her permission if she has reached puberty. A virgin's silence is considered as consent.

Forced sex
The wife must have sex whenever her husband demands it.

M5.1 It is obligatory for a woman to let her husband have sex with her immediately when:
(a) He asks her;
(b) At home;
(c) She can physically endure it.

Wife Beating
The Koran says that a wife can be beaten. Mohammed recommended wife beating in his last sermon at Mecca. Here is the Sharia:

DEALING WITH A REBELLIOUS WIFE
M10.12 When a husband notices signs of rebelliousness in his wife whether in words as when she answers him coldly when she used to do so politely. or he asks her to come to bed and she refuses, contrary to her usual habit; or whether in acts, as when he finds her averse to him when she was previously kind and cheerful), he warns her in words without keeping from her or hitting her, for it may be that she has an excuse.
The warning could be to tell her,
"Fear Allah concerning the rights you owe to me,"
or it could be to explain that rebelliousness nullifies his obligation to support her and give her a turn amongst other wives, or it could be to inform her,
"Your obeying me is religiously obligatory".
If she commits rebelliousness, he keeps from sleeping (having sex) with her without words and may hit her, but not in a way that injures

her, meaning he may not bruise her, break bones, wound her, or cause blood to flow. It is unlawful to strike another's face. He may hit her whether she is rebellious only once or whether more than once, though a weaker opinion holds that he may not hit her unless there is repeated rebelliousness.

How does this affect the birth rate in a Muslim society?

1) Since Sharia Law follows the example of Mohammed, the minimum age for marriage should be nine years old. The Saudi Arabian Government is currently[10] trying to introduce a minimum age for marriage of sixteen years old. This is probably through a mixture of embarrassment and international pressure. It is facing stiff opposition from that country's all powerful religious authorities however (at the present time there is no minimum age for marriage in Saudi Arabia[11]).

2) In Islamic societies, a family's honour is all important and depends largely on the pristine morals of its female members. Marrying off daughters as early as possible reduces the chance of sexual impropriety before marriage.

3) Girls have little say in this matter.

4) Once married a girl has no right to refuse sexual intercourse with her husband except under extreme circumstances.

5) Contraception in Islamic societies is frowned upon. Islam promotes large families as being highly desirable.

6) Predestination is a core belief in Islam. Everything has been planned by Allah and whatever we do will not change his plan. Worrying about providing for children is therefore not an issue for Muslims. When asked about who will provide for their children, a common reply is, "Allah will provide".

7) A Muslim may have up to four wives. A woman of child bearing age whose husband dies for any reason will usually be expected to remarry. In the event of a war involving a Muslim group in which three quarters of the Muslim men are killed, the birth rate will not be affected too much.

In theory then, a woman may be married at nine and kept pregnant constantly from then on. By twenty years old, when a non-Muslim girl might be expecting her first child, a Muslim girl could have ten

---

[10] 2013

[11] http://globalpublicsquare.blogs.cnn.com/2013/05/27/will-saudi-arabia-end-child-marriage

children and be expecting her first grandchild. The reality is of course far less than this. High infant mortality and the death of mothers is just one limiting factor. In some Islamic countries this is exacerbated, perversely, by lack of "birth spacing."

Whilst none of these points is necessarily mandatory, Islam exerts a higher degree of control over its followers than most other religions. The Catholic Church also promotes a high birth rate yet in Italy, the home of the church, the birth rate is one of the lowest in the world. In a society ruled by Sharia Law the pressure to follow these rules will be very strong. Even for Muslims living in Western countries however, we can see the results. In France, an estimated 10% of the population are Muslims. Of children born there however, almost one third are Muslims. With the baby boomers starting to die off, expect huge demographic changes across the Western World. These will favour Muslim populations.

Whilst not all Islamic countries are currently promoting unchecked population growth, the trend can be seen quite clearly from a brief look at global population statistics.

Associated Press Gaza[12]

Hanan Suelem wanted an abortion after the 7th pregnancy, but Islamic clerics told her that she would be "killing a soul." She told them that her soul was dying. "After this, no more, never," she said, speaking almost in a whisper. "I have learned now about the IUD." The area's schools operate on two and three shifts to accommodate the growing Palestinian population. Gaza's population of 1.1 million is expected to double by 2014. Half are under age 15. It is already a highly congested area with few jobs, severely inadequate housing and almost no natural resources. The West Bank and Gaza combined have a population of over 3 million, which is expected to rise to 5.5 million in 14 years. The fertility rate is seven children per woman. Almost all the babies survive and adults live to an average of 73. Many young Palestinians do not want their children to suffer as they did in oversized poor families, but large families are not only traditional, but a point of nationalist pride and as a way to outnumber the Israelis on the land the two groups share. Fortunately, health and education officials quietly support family planning through clinics and community outreach services. Women are taught about the different methods of contraception that are acceptable under Islam -- anything

---

[12] February 24, 2000 NY Times. Cramped Gaza Multiplies at unrivalled Rate.

except permanent means, like sterilization or tubal ligation. The IUD and birth control pills are growing in favour. Health officials refer delicately to the "spacing" of children, since the suggestion to place limits on family size would violate Islamic teaching. Women are told that it is written in the Koran that God orders women to breast-feed for two years. Women in the West Bank average 5.6 children per woman, compared to Israel, with about 2.7 children, the worldwide average. Gaza grows at over 4% a year while Israel grows only 2% a year, which includes high levels of immigration. Palestinian advocates are pushing for a law that would raise the legal age of marriage, since half of Palestinian women marry before they reach age 18 and it is legal for them to marry at 15 in Gaza and 17 in the West Bank.

Author's note:

In 1948 there were around 170,000 Arab refugees, (these refugees were not referred to as "Palestinians" at that time). Today, there are around 5 Million. Whilst this is partly due to territorial gains by Israel, the increase is still huge.

7 Jihad Begins

Mohammed had now gained effective control over the tribes of Medina. He quickly turned his attention back to the Quraysh of Mecca. The caravans that supplied Mecca from the North came close to Medina and Mohammed began sending out war parties to attack them. These caravans were usually well armed and the first seven attempts were unsuccessful. All the tribes of Arabia had an agreement at that time. During the four holy months, fighting of any sort was taboo. This was probably to facilitate the trade on which the Arabs depended for their livelihoods. During these months, large or costly items could be moved around without expensive armed guards. This benefited everybody and was therefore rigidly adhered to.

On the last day of one these months, a Muslim raiding party came across a Meccan caravan. The next day they would be free to attack the caravan. Unfortunately for them, by this time the caravan would be within the boundaries of Mecca. Within these boundaries fighting was forbidden at any time, since Mecca was a holy city. They were in a quandary as to what to do. Eventually, they decided to attack the caravan anyway.

For the benefit of the sceptics amongst you, (scepticism is good) I am going to quote (with the kind permission of Bill Warner), from *Mohammed and the Unbelievers*. I have included the relevant pages of *The Sira*, faithfully translated from the original as *The Life of Muhammad* by Prof. A Guillaume. If you compare the two you will see that *Mohammed and the Unbelievers* is clearer and easier to read. Importantly, it doesn't leave out anything important or distort the truth in any way. For this reason I will mostly quote from this book from here on in.

From *The Sira*:

1425 The Muslims took council. They were faced with a dilemma: if they attacked the caravan now, they would be killing in a sacred month. Luckily, the sacred month ended that day and the next day there would be no taboo about killing. But there was another problem: by nightfall they would be in the sacred area of Mecca. In the sanctified area, there could never be any killing. They hesitated and talked about what to do. They decided to kill as many as possible and take their goods before the next day.

1425 Islam drew first blood against the Quraysh of Mecca. They attacked the unarmed men. Amr, the first man to be killed by Jihad, was shot by an arrow. One man escaped and they captured two others. The Muslims took the enemies' camels with their goods and headed back to Medina and Mohammed. On the way they talked about how Mohammed would get one fifth of the stolen goods.

1425 When they got back, Mohammed said he had not ordered them to attack in the sacred month. He detained the caravan and the two prisoners and refused to do anything with them or the goods. The prisoners said, "Mohammed has violated the sacred month, shed blood therein, stolen goods, and taken prisoners." But the Koran said:

2:217 When they ask you about fighting in the holy month, say: Fighting at this time is a serious offense, but it is worse in Allah's eyes to deny others the path to Him, to disbelieve in Him and to drive His worshippers out of the Sacred Mosque. Idolatry is a greater sin than murder. They will not stop fighting you until you turn away from your religion. But any of you who renounce your faith and die a Kaffir will have your works count for nothing in this world and the world to come. These people will be prisoners of the Fire, where they will live forever.

1426 According to Mohammed, to resist the doctrine of Islam and persuade Muslims to drop their faith was worse than killing. Before Islam, the rule of justice in Arabia was a killing for a killing, but now to resist Islam was worse than murder. Those who argued against Islam and resisted Islam could be killed as a sacred act. So the murder and theft were sanctified. The spoils of war were distributed and a ransom was set for the prisoners. The men who had killed and stolen were now concerned about whether they would get their share of the spoils. So once again the Koran spoke:

2:218 Those who believe and those who have fled their countries and have fought for Allah's cause [Jihad] may hope for His mercy; Allah is forgiving and merciful.

I426 As Muslims who had been exiled and fought they were blessed by Allah. They received their spoils of war and Mohammed took his 20 percent.

From *Bukhari's Hadith*:
B4,53,351 Allah's Apostle said, "The spoils of war have been made legal for me."

A war poem from *The Sira*:
You [Quraysh] count war in the holy month a grave matter
but graver is your opposition to Mohammed and your unbelief.
Though you defame us for killing Amr our lances drank Amr's blood.
We lit the flame of war. —Abu Bakr (Mohammed's right hand man)

Jihad, the New Kind of Warfare
Before he moved to Medina, Mohammed had never used violence. Now that he had the means, he began to attack the Meccans, who had spurned his calls to Islam.

On the face of it, this was simply an attack by a tribal leader; (Mohammed) to steal goods from a group of rivals. In fact this was the start of a war which Mohammed and his followers would wage against all of his enemies (the Kaffirs) forever.

As this war progressed, Mohammed would develop a strategy for an entirely new system of warfare, which he called Jihad. Westerners translate Jihad as "holy war" but it is in fact far more than this. Mohammed was a very capable military tactician. Jihad however, barely concerns itself with military tactics. Had it done so, Jihad would have been rendered obsolete as soon as it encountered newer and more effective military technologies, such as crossbows or guns.

Warfare, like all types of violent coercion, has a psychological aspect to it. In many ways, this is more important than the actual violence itself. Mohammed's genius was to understand this psychology and incorporate it into the tactics of Jihad. Because of this, Jihad is effective when fighting with bows and arrows or laser guided rockets. As the story unfolds, we will see how the strategy of Jihad was developed and applied. I will begin to list these as they appear:

Rules of Jihad:

1) Jihad is sanctioned by Allah. There is no higher authority; therefore it is always justified.

2) Never abide by any rules or limitations. The ends justify ANY means no matter how shocking. Jihad can be any action which advances Islam or weakens the Kaffirs whether by a group or an individual. Even donating money to pay for someone else's Jihad is a type of Jihad itself.

3) ALWAYS play the victim. Mohammed twisted his situation around. Although he had attacked innocent people without provocation he blamed them. He said that they had "stopped others from becoming Muslims" and had worshiped idols. The attack was their fault and the Muslims were the victims, not the Kaffirs.

4) Keep repeating this and people will eventually begin to believe it. If you can persuade the victim to accept the blame you have won, because retaliation requires a sense of injustice. If the victim accepts the blame they will turn their hatred towards themselves.

The Bible contains acts of war by the Jews against their enemies which were approved of by their God. This approval was applied only to specific battles and specific instances in history. It was not part of an ongoing strategy to take over the world. The God of the Bible did not give approval for relentless, unprovoked violence against unbelievers.

Direct Translation from the Original Arabic text (*The Sira*) by Professor Guillaume:

EXPEDITION OF ABDULLAH B. JAHSH AND THE COMING DOWN OF "THEY WILL ASK YOU ABOUT THE SACRED MONTH"

The apostle sent Abdullah b. Jahsh b. Ri'ab al-Asadi in Rijab on his return from the first Badr. He sent with him eight emigrants[Ed. The Meccan Muslims who fled to Medina with Mohammed], without any of the Ansar[Ed. The Medinan Muslims who welcomed Mohammed to live with them after his flight from Mecca]. He wrote for him a letter and ordered him not to look at it until he had journeyed for two days, and to do what he was ordered to do but not to put pressure on any of his companions. The names of the eight Emigrants were, Abu Hudhayfa, Abdullah b. Jabsh, Ukkasha b Mibsan, Utba b Ghazwan, Sa'd b. Abu Waqqas, Amir b. Rabi'a, Waqid b Abdullah, and Khalid b. al-Bukayr. When Abdullah had travelled for two days he opened the letter and looked into it, and this is what it said: "When you have read this letter of mine proceed until you reach Nakhla between Mecca and Al-Ta'if. Lie in wait there for Quraysh and find out for us what they are doing." Having read the letter he said, "To hear is to obey." Then he said to his companions, "The apostle has commanded me to go to Nakhla to lie in wait there for Quraysh so as to bring him news of them. He has forbidden me to put pressure on any of you, so if anyone wishes for martyrdom, let him go forward, and he who does not, let him go back; as for me, I am going on as the prophet has ordered." So he went on, as did all his companions, not one of them falling back. He journeyed along the Hijaz until at a mine called Babran above al-Furu, Sa'd and Utba lost the camel which they were riding by turns, so they stayed behind to look for it, while Abdullah and the rest of them went on to Nakhla. A caravan of Quraysh carrying dry raisins and leather and other merchandise of Quraysh passed by them, Amr b al-Hadrami (349), Uthman b Abdullah b Mughira and his brother Naufal the Makhzumites and al-Hakam b Kaysan, freedman of Hisham b. al-Mughira being among them. When the caravan saw them they were afraid of them because they had camped near them. Ukkasha who had shaved his head looked down on them and when they saw him they felt safe and said, "They are pilgrims, you have nothing to fear from them." Then they encouraged each other and decided to kill as many as they could of them and take what they had. Waqid shot Amr b. al-Hadrami with an arrow and killed him, and

Uthman and Al-Hakam surrendered. Naufal escaped and eluded them. Abdullah and his companions took the caravan and the two prisoners and came to Medina with them. One of Abdullah's family mentioned that he said to his companions, "A fifth of what we have taken belongs to the apostle" (This was before God had appointed one fifth of the booty to him.) So he set apart for the apostle a fifth of the caravan and divided the rest among his companions. When they came to the apostle, he said, "I did not order you to fight in the sacred month and he held the caravan and the two prisoners in suspense and refused to take anything from them. When the apostle said that, the men were in despair and thought that they were doomed. Their Muslim bretheren reproached them for what they had done, and the Quraysh said "Mohammed and his companions have violated the sacred month, shed blood therein, taken booty and captured men." The Muslims in Mecca who opposed them said that they had done it in Shaban. The Jews turned this raid into an omen against the apostle. "Amr g al-Hadrami whom Waqid had killed they said meant "amarate'l-harb" (war has come to life), al-Hadrami means "hadrati'l-harb" (means war is present) and Waqid meant "wugadati'l-harb", (war is kindled); but God turned this against them, not for them, and when there was much talk about it God sent down to his apostle: they will ask you about the sacred month and war in it. Say, war therein is a serious matter, but keeping people from the way of God and disbelieving in him and in the sacred Mosque and driving out his people there from is more serious with God. i.e. if you have killed in the sacred month they have kept you back from the way of God with their unbelief in him, and from the sacred Mosque, and have driven you from it when you were its people. This is a more serious matter with God and the killing of those of them whom you have slain. And seduction is worse than killing. i.e. they used to seduce the Muslim in his religion until they made him return to unbelief after believing and this is worse with God than killing. And they will not cease to fight you until they turn you back from your religion if they can. I.e. they are doing more heinous acts than that contumaciously. And when the Koran came down about that, God relieved the Muslims of their anxiety in the matter, the apostle took the caravan and the prisoners. Quraysh sent to him to redeem Uthman and and al-Hakam and the apostles said, "we will not let you redeem them until our two companions come meaning Sa'd and Utba, for we fear for them on your account. If you kill them, we will kill your two friends." So when Sa'd and Utba turned up the apostle let them redeem them. As for al-

Hakam he became a good Muslim and stayed with the apostle until he was killed as a martyr at Bi'rMa'una. Uthman went back to Mecca and died there as an unbeliever. When Abdullah and his companions were relieved of their anxiety when the Koran came down, they were anxious for reward, and said, "can we hope that it will count as a raid for which we shall be given the reward of combatants?" so God sent down concerning him: "those who believe and have emigrated and fought in the way of God, these may hope for God's mercy, for God is forgiving and merciful." That is, God gave them the greatest hopes there in. The tradition about this comes from al-Zuhri and Yazidb.Ruman from Urwa b al-Zubayr. One of Abdullah's family mentioned that God divided the booty when he made it permissible and gave up four fifths to whom God had allowed to take it and one fifth to God and his apostle. So it remained on the basis of what Abdullah had done with the booty of that caravan.

Abu Bakr said concerning Abdullah's raid [though others say that Abdulla himself said it], when Quraysh said, "Muhammad and his companions have broken the sacred month shed blood therein and taken booty and made prisoners".

You count war in the holy month a grave matter, but graver is, if one judges rightly, your opposition to Muhammad's teaching, and your unbelief in it, which God sees and witnesses. Your driving God's people from his mosque so that none can be seen worshiping him there. Though you defame us for killing him, more dangerous to Islam is the sinner who envies. Our lances drank of Ibn al-Hadrami's blood. In Nakhla when Waqid lit the flame of war, Uthhman Ibn Abdullah is with us, a leather hand, streaming with blood restrains him.

8 The Battle of Badr

A large caravan was on its way back to Mecca, loaded with goods and treasure. Mohammed heard of this and decided to attack the caravan and steal the treasure. Some of his men were reluctant to get involved, as the Quraysh were their relatives and tribal kin. Killing them had always been forbidden before the time of Islam, but now was made lawful by Allah. Mohammed set out with a small army to attack the caravan, but the Meccans found out. They sent a fast rider to Mecca to call for assistance. In Mecca, an army was quickly assembled. They marched north to defend the caravan. The caravan however, managed to avoid Mohammed's army and sneak through to safety. The caravan was out of harm's way but the Meccan army still decided to take on the Muslims at a place called Badr.

Until now Mohammed's fighters had never fought a real battle. So far most of their targets had been small trading caravans. The Muslims were heavily outnumbered, but before the battle began, Mohammed had a revelation which is recorded in *The Sira*:

1445 Some arrows flew and one Muslim was killed. Mohammed addressed his army. "By Allah, every man who is slain this day by fighting with courage and advancing, not retreating will enter Paradise." One of his men who had been eating dates said, "You mean there is nothing between me and Paradise except being killed by the Quraysh?" He flung the dates to the side, picked up his sword, and set out to fight. He got his wish and was later killed.
1445 One of Mohammed's men asked what made Allah laugh. Mohammed answered, "When a warrior plunges into the midst of the enemy without armour." The man removed his coat of mail, picked up his sword, and made ready to attack [and he was killed].

31

The Muslims gained great courage from Mohammed's revelation. Not only were they no longer afraid of death, they actually welcomed it. Should they win the fight, the spoils of war would be theirs; if they lost they would attain Paradise.

The battle went well for the Muslims and as luck would have it, a dust storm appeared at the decisive moment. It blew straight into the eyes of the Meccans. According to Mohammed, this was the angels blowing sand in the face of their enemies. The Muslims were victorious in their first ever battle against great odds. Mohammed was a very capable military tactician. It was his ability to motivate his followers to suicidal bravery which was his real genius however.

From *The Sira*:
1455 As the bodies were dragged to the well, one of the Muslims saw the body of his father thrown in. He said, "My father was a virtuous, wise, kind, and cultured man. I had hoped he would become a Muslim, but he died a Kaffir. His abode is Hell-fire forever." Before Islam, killing of kin and tribal brothers had been forbidden since the dawn of time. After Islam, brother would kill brother and sons would kill fathers fighting in Allah's cause: Jihad.

Author's Comments:
The participants of this battle numbered only in the hundreds. It is however, probably one of the most important battles in history. It marks the turning point for a religion which numbers over 1 billion souls today. To Muslims it is very well known and yet Westerners remain almost totally ignorant of this event. Mohammed's men went into this fight as a rag tag bunch of brigands. They marched out as a potent political force. The success of Mohammed was news all around Arabia. His success (and war booty) began to attract more followers.

Importantly, Mohammed added another plank to his new system of Jihad. By introducing the concept of martyrdom into his religion, (/political movement) he managed to inspire his followers to suicidal bravery. This is a huge advantage to any fighting force. It is particularly useful to one which can replace fallen warriors as quickly as Islam. Mohammed clearly understood the advantage this gave him. Much of his teaching from this point on would be woven around the importance of martyrdom. He spoke repeatedly of the rewards which await shahid (martyrs) in the afterlife. These far outshine anything an ordinary Muslim can expect. There are seven different layers in the Islamic heaven. The difference between one layer and another is as

32

great as the difference between the earth and the first level. The shahid go straight to the Seventh Heaven.

Rules of Jihad:
5)   Inspire your followers to fanatical suicidal bravery.

9 Abrogation of the Koran

Whilst he lived in Mecca, Mohammed was surrounded by enemies. Although he made threats at that time, he was never violent. Now he was a political force and set about making good on those threats. The Koran clearly reflects this change. It is therefore divided by scholars into the Koran of Mecca and the Koran of Medina. Because it is not arranged chronologically, this distinction is hard for a layman to recognize. Once you arrange the Koran in its correct chronological order however it becomes very clear.

From the Koran of Mecca:
88:21 Warn them, because you [Mohammed] are merely a warner. You have no authority over them, but whoever turns back and disbelieves, Allah will punish them terribly.

Compare this with the later Koran of Medina:
8:12 Then your Lord spoke to His angels and said, "I will be with you. Give strength to the believers. I will send terror into the Kaffir's hearts, cut off their heads and even the tips of their fingers!" This was because they opposed Allah and His messenger. Ones who oppose Allah and His messenger will be severely punished by Allah. We said, "This is for you! Taste it and know that the Kaffirs will receive the torment of the Fire."

Mohammed made it clear that wherever there was a contradiction in the Koran; the earlier verse would be abrogated (cancelled out) by the later verse. Since the Koran is not written in chronological order, it is impossible to understand it without knowing which verses have been abrogated. Muslims often point to non-violent quotes from the

Meccan Koran, but fail to point out that these verses have been abrogated by later ones.

I want you to put on your thinking cap at this point, because I am about to explain a very important facet of Islam which is a little challenging. This is however very important for understanding Islam itself.

As we have just seen, later verses of the Koran abrogate earlier ones. We already know however, that the Koran is considered to be the perfect word of Allah. In Western logic, when two things contradict each other, one of them must be wrong. In Islamic logic however, two things can contradict each other and yet both be right.

The Koran tells Muslims to follow the example of Mohammed but which example? In Mecca, Mohammed never used violence against Kaffirs and in the very early days even showed some tolerance of other religions. Once in Medina, Mohammed used violence almost all the time to achieve his aims. He never showed any tolerance to Kaffirs at all.

The Medina Koran is the later one and so abrogates the Meccan Koran and yet the Meccan Koran is still valid because the Koran (and Mohammed) is perfect. So a Muslim can follow either example, though the Medina example is better because it is later. So how does a Muslim know which one to choose? As usual we have to look at Mohammed's example to know the answer. In Mecca, Mohammed was not powerful and was surrounded by enemies. During that time he preached some tolerance and non-violence. When he went to Medina, he became powerful and used violence frequently to achieve his goals.

Mohammed's example of how to behave is not consistent but varies according to circumstance. When you are not in a position of power, be quiet and do not draw attention to yourself. Use the time to build up strength and numbers until you become powerful enough to begin Jihad. This is Mohammed's example or "Sunnah", which comes from the hadith (traditions of Mohammed) and *The Sira* (his biography).

10 War is Deceit

By this time Mohammed had clearly realised the tactical advantage of unflinching bravery amongst his warriors. As a religious leader, he was able to offer his followers threats and inducements in the afterlife which most military commanders cannot. He set down further rules such as this one from *The Sira*.

1477 When a Muslim met a Kaffir in war, he was not to turn his back except as a tactical manoeuvre. A Muslim fighting in Allah's cause had to face the enemy. Not doing so brought on the wrath of Allah and the judgment of Hell. Fear was not an option for a Jihadist.

The terms of Jihad were laid down at this time and are also recorded in Ishaq's biography:

1480 If those who practiced the old religions submitted to Islam, all would be forgiven. But if not, they were to take a lesson from Badr. The Jihad would not stop until Kaffirs surrendered to Islam. Only submission to Islam would save the Kaffirs.

The Koran backs this up:
8:38 Tell the Kaffirs that if they change their ways, then they will be forgiven for their past. If, however, they continue to sin, let them remember the fate of those who came before them. Fight against them until they stop persecuting you, and Allah's religion reigns sovereign over all others. If they cease, Allah knows all they do, but if they turn their backs, know that Allah is your protector—an excellent helper.

Author's Comments:

Mohammed made it clear that his enemies had two choices, to submit to his will or fight against his suicidal followers forever. Threatening people to submit or be killed was hardly a new concept, even in Mohammed's day. The real genius of Jihad however, lies in its use of deceit. Mohammed used it to confuse his enemies and to make them believe that he could be negotiated with. In fact he was sworn to fight them until they either submitted or died.

Mohammed divided the world into two parts, Dar al Islam and Dar al Harb. Dar al Islam was the land of Islam, which had submitted and was ruled by Sharia law. Dar al Harb on the other hand was the land of war which was all the other parts of the globe. Nations may not think that they are at war with Islam, but if they are not ruled by Sharia Law, then Islam is in fact at war with them.

All Muslims are part of a nation known as The Ummah, which is at war with all other nations. Whilst hostilities may not be happening at a given moment, they are still technically at war, even though the ordinary Muslims may not know it.

This peace is temporary and is known in Islam as "Hudna." A Muslim who lives in England is not therefore an Englishman who happens to be a Muslim. He is instead, a Muslim who happens to live in England. All of his loyalties lie first and foremost with the Ummah which is technically at war with the UK.

It is the ability of Islam to hide these facts from non-Muslims which makes Jihad so successful. Muslim leaders understand this and they expend a good deal of their resources in promoting this deception. We have already seen the way in which the Islamic holy books are presented in order to make their interpretation as difficult as possible. Later on we will see in greater depth, the ways in which political Islam works tirelessly to perpetuate this deception.

This is the next and arguably the most important tactic of Jihad.

Rules of Jihad:

6) Deceive the enemy (the Kaffirs) whenever possible in order to secure victory.

Mohammed not only used deceit frequently but as we will see he was a master of it.

Whilst we are on the subject of deceit, please note the use of the word "persecuted" in the above Koranic quote. It may seem strange to us that Mohammed was in the middle of attacking his enemies, whilst at the same time complaining of persecution. Mohammed redefined the word "persecuting" to mean those who would not allow Sharia law to rule over them. In other words, Islam is supposed to rule over the whole world, so those who oppose this are "persecuting" Muslims, even when they are being attacked by them.

Words are very powerful things. Words define thoughts so twisting words can alter the way people think. Be aware that if you are opposed to the introduction of Sharia Law to rule over your society; then you are considered to be persecuting Muslims. Because of this, Islam considers it legitimate to attack you. Islamic doctrine regards this as "self-defence". Furthermore, Kaffirs killed by Jihad are not considered to be "innocent" victims. We frequently hear Muslim spokespeople insist that killing "innocent" victims is against Islamic teaching except in self-defence. What they do not explain, is the different concept of the terms "innocent" and "self-defence" in Islamic teaching.

11 The First Tribe of Jews

The spoils of the Battle of Badr were divided up with Mohammed taking his usual twenty percent cut. This was, and of course remains, the basis for dividing the spoils of Jihad (the spiritual leader gets twenty percent). Mohammed's followers now began to acquire both wealth and power. This made his religion far more attractive to the desert Arabs. They now began to swell the ranks of his followers even more.

After the Battle of Badr, Mohammed made a few armed raids on tribes allied to the Meccans. He then turned his attention to one of the Jewish tribes of Medina.

THE AFFAIR OF THE JEWS OF QAYNUQA
I545 there were three tribes of Jews in medina. The Banu Qaynuqa were Goldsmiths and lived in a stronghold. Mohammed said they had broken the treaty signed when Mohammed came to Medina. How they did this is unclear.

I545 Mohammed assembled the Jews in their market and said, "O Jews, be careful that Allah does not bring vengeance upon you the way he did to the Quraysh. Become Muslims. You know that I am the prophet that was sent to you. You will find that in your scriptures."

I545 they replied, "Oh Mohammed, you seem to think that we are your people. Don't fool yourself. You may have killed a few merchants of the Quraysh, but we are men of war and real men."

I545 the response of The Koran:
3:12 say to the Kaffirs, "Soon you will be defeated and thrown into hell, a wretched home!" Truly, there has been a sign for you in the two armies which met in battle. One army fought for Allah's cause, and the other Army was a group of Kaffirs, and the Kaffirs saw with

39

their own eyes that their enemy was twice its actual size. Allah gives help to whom he pleases. Certainly there is a lesson to be learned in this for those who recognize it.

1546 a little later, Mohammed besieged the Jewish tribe of Banu Qaynuqa in their quarters. Neither of the other two Jewish tribes came to their support. Finally, the Jews surrendered and expected to be slaughtered after their capture.
1546 an Arab ally, bound to them by a client relationship, approached Mohammed and said, "O Mohammed, deal kindly with my clients." Mohammed ignored him. The ally repeated the request and Mohammed still ignored him. The ally grabbed Mohammed by the robe and enraged Mohammed, Who said, "let me go!" The ally said, "No, you must deal kindly with my clients. They have protected me and now you would kill them all? I fear these changes."

The response by *The Koran*:
5:57O, you who believe, do not take those who have received the Scriptures [Jews and Christians] before you, who have scoffed and jested at your religion, or who are Kaffirs for your friends. Fear Allah if you are true believers. When you call to prayer, they make it a mockery and a joke. This is because they are a people who do not understand

Author's Comments:
It is a core belief of Islam that the Koran is the perfect word of Allah. The Koran instructs Muslims very clearly, not to take non-Muslims as their friends. They may be friendly towards Kaffirs, particularly in order to gain an advantage for Islam. However, the extent to which a Muslim is a true friend of a Kaffir is the extent to which he is not a Muslim.

When you are trying to motivate a group of people to commit violent acts against another group, it is important to break ties between them. Any military commander would understand this concept.

During the first Christmas of WW1, the English and German soldiers came out of the trenches, sang carols and shared cigarettes and food. The powers that be, made sure that this never happened again. To motivate people to violence; it is important to demonize and de-humanize your opponents and Mohammed did this constantly. He never referred to human beings as a whole but divided the world into

Muslims and Kaffirs. Kaffirs are described as the worst kind of creature and any action against them is justified.

The Sira goes on to describe how at this time, Mohammed encouraged his followers to assassinate his enemies and critics. He allowed and even encouraged, them to use deceit in order to achieve their aims. Often, they would gain the trust of their enemies in order to murder them.

From *The Sira*:

I554 The Apostle of Allah said, "Kill any Jew who falls into your power." Hearing this, Muhayyisa fell upon a Jewish merchant who was a business associate and killed him. Muhayyisa's brother was not a Muslim and asked how Muhayyisa could kill a man who had been his friend and partner in many business deals. The Muslim said that if Mohammed had asked him to kill his brother he would have done it immediately. His brother said "You mean that if Mohammed said to cut off my head you would do it?" "Yes," was the reply. The older brother then said, "By Allah, any religion that brings you to this is marvellous." And he decided then and there to become a Muslim.

It is surprising what most people are capable of. In experiment after experiment, psychologists have found that when a group deems behaviour to be acceptable, the vast majority will go along with things which "civilized" people might consider "inhuman".

How many Japanese people would think twice before eating whale? How many Vietnamese people would think it wrong to kill and eat a dog? In the early nineties half a million Rwandans were brutally hacked to death with machetes by their compatriots. In the forties six million Jews were wiped out in Europe, mostly by ordinary German folk. Closer to home, in my grandmothers day, children of five or six were being sent up chimneys to clean them, many would never return.

To a modern Western mind these things are abhorrent and yet people just like us are quite capable of doing them. Religions have an especially powerful influence on societies. When people believe they have authority from a divine ruler, they are capable of overriding normal human feelings of revulsion. When "everyone else is doing it too," even the most extreme behaviour becomes easy to justify.

Mohammed was not only a religious leader. The acts which he carried out from here until his death are almost all of a political nature. Through Jihad he became king of all Arabia within just nine years.

The political aspects of Islam bear many similarities with the political aspects of communism or fascism. Such ideologies are very dangerous. Small but fanatical groups which number little more than 5% of the population can seize power with devastating consequences. Once they have power it is often impossible to prize it from them without outside assistance.

Communism lasted around 70 years, Fascism barely a decade but Islam has been around for 1400 years and today is stronger than ever.

12 The Battle of Uhud

After the Battle of Badr the Meccans wanted revenge. They raised an army and marched to Medina. There they camped outside of the town waiting for the Muslims. Mohammed wanted to wait until the Meccans attacked the town. He figured he could use it for a defence. Many of his hot-headed warriors now felt invincible however. They wanted to march out to meet them. Mohammed finally agreed and marched out with his men to meet the Meccans at a place called Uhud.

The battle began well for the Muslims, who now fought with suicidal bravery. They believed that death would lead them to Paradise. In the heat of the battle, the Meccans were cut off from their camp which held their supplies and valuables.

Mohammed had set a group of archers to protect his rear. Seeing that the Meccans were cut off from their camp, these archers ran forward. They wanted to be first to grab the booty. This left Mohammed's army exposed and the Meccan cavalry charged smashing apart the Muslim's defences.

Mohammed had to run for his life and his army was soundly defeated. Fortunately for him, the Meccans did not press their advantage. They had come for tribal justice and this had been extracted. Like most human societies which resort to violence, the Meccans had an objective. Once this objective had been achieved, they put down their weapons and went back to their lives.

For many Muslims, the defeat at Uhud was a stark reality check. They had believed that Allah was behind them and they were therefore invincible. Mohammed, cunning as ever, used the setback to his advantage.

He explained to the Muslims that Allah was testing them. If he gave them nothing but easy victories, Allah would never see who his true followers were. It was also important for the Muslims to learn that they were fighting primarily for the glory of Allah and the advancement of Islam. The spoils of war were really just fringe benefits. Concentrating on the pleasures of this life had caused them to be defeated. Allah was displeased with them.

From the Koran:
3:140 If you have been wounded, be certain that the same has already befallen your enemies. We bring misfortune to mankind in turns so that Allah can discern who are the true believers and so that we may select Martyrs from among you. Allah does not love those who do evil.
3:142 Did you think that you would be permitted into Paradise before Allah tested you to see who would fight for his cause [Jihad] and endure until the end?

Author's Comments:
   In war, one of the most important factors for victory is to maintain good morale amongst your troops. When you are having constant successes this is easy, but a string of defeats can cause soldiers to give up hope and lose the will to fight.
   Mohammed, with his usual brilliance, gave his fighters divine inspiration to fight through victory or defeat. Don't fight just for victory he told them, Allah has assured us of that; fight so that Allah can judge your devotion to him and he will reward you with Paradise. This is the next rule of Jihad, which ensures that Muslim fighters always have high morale, even when they are in a hopeless situation.

Rules of Jihad:
   7) Never ever give up, even when you are being beaten.

   After the battle of Uhud, Mohammed once again sent out assassins to kill the leader of a group who opposed him. With Mohammed's blessing they deceived the man into believing that they were friends, using his trust to get close enough to kill him. Mohammed used this type of deceitful operation many times to kill political opponents.

From *The Sira*:
1681 One of the Ghatafans approached Mohammed saying he was a Muslim but no one else knew it. Mohammed told him, "Go and sow distrust among our enemies. War is deceit."

And from *Bukhari's Hadith*:
B4,52,268 Mohammed said, "War is deceit."

Mohammed was a master of psychology and regularly used deceit to gain advantage over his enemies. He also encouraged his followers to do the same.

13 The Second Tribe of Jews

The second of the Jewish tribes in Medina were becoming alarmed by Mohammed's growing power and aggression. They began to hatch a plot against Mohammed. Unfortunately for them, Mohammed always had excellent intelligence. He heard of this and laid siege to their fort.

These Jews were farmers who grew very fine date palms. Mohammed burnt down many of these palm trees which incensed the Jews. They called out, "You have prohibited wanton destruction and blamed those who do that. Now you do what you forbid."

The Jews were helpless however and cut a deal with Mohammed. They were allowed to leave with whatever they could carry, except for their armour and weapons. They even tore down their houses to take the wooden beams. These were valuable in Arabia where no trees grow. Since there was no fighting, Mohammed took 100% of the spoils. He spent this on his family and buying weapons for Jihad.

To answer his critics, *The Koran* brought down some new revelations. It was Allah who had wreaked vengeance which was the fault of the Jews.

From *The Koran*:
59:2 It was He who caused the People of the Book [the Jews] to leave their homes and go into the first exile. They did not think they would leave, and they thought that their fortresses could protect them from Allah. But Allah's wrath reached them from where they did not expect it and cast terror into their hearts, so that they destroyed their homes with their own hands, as well as by the hands of the believers. Take warning from this example, you who have the eyes to see it!

From Bukhari:
B4,52,153 Because the property of the Jews that Allah had given to Mohammed had not been won by the Muslims through the use of their horses and camels, it belonged exclusively to Mohammed. He used it to give his family their yearly allowance and he spent the rest on weapons and horses for Jihad.

And *The Sira*:
I654 The Jews were very fortunate that Allah let them go with a few worldly processions. They got out alive and Allah did not slay them, but they would burn in Hell since they resisted Mohammed

Author's Comments:
   Since the Kaffirs were the enemies of Allah, anything that Mohammed did to them was always justified. His doctrine of Jihad was taking shape as total warfare against the Kaffirs. He would accept no limitations on his ability to wage war against them. Allah would always provide justification for whatever rules he broke. Mohammed had now been in Medina for around three years.

14 The Battle of the Trench

Another group of Jews decided to take on Mohammed to destroy him. They made an allegiance between the Meccans and another large tribe of Arabs and set out for Medina. Mohammed received news of this from his spies and immediately set about fortifying the weaker parts of Medina with a large trench. When the Jews and their allies arrived, they could not get past the trench and laid siege to the town.

The remaining Jewish tribe in Medina was persuaded, although reluctantly, to make an alliance with the attacking tribes. As usual, Mohammed got to hear all about this, (he always had excellent intelligence). He sent some of his spies to sow discord between the attackers. This they did very successfully. They deceived each side into believing that the others could not be trusted. Eventually the Meccans gave up. They were running out of food and water and decided to go back home. Mohammed immediately turned his attention to the remaining Jewish tribe of Medina.

From *The Sira*:
1684 Mohammed called upon his troops and they headed for the Jews. Mohammed rode up to the forts and called out, "You brothers of apes, has Allah disgraced you and brought His vengeance upon you."

The Jews had no choice. They could convert to Islam, or they could surrender and face Mohammed's judgment. They did not want to convert and so Mohammed chose one of his lieutenants to make a judgment for him.

From Bukhari:
B5,58,148 When some of the remaining Jews of Medina agreed to obey a verdict from Saed, Mohammed sent for him. He approached

the mosque riding a donkey and Mohammed said, "Stand up for your leader." Mohammed then said, "Saed, give these people your verdict." Saed replied, "Their soldiers should be beheaded, and their women and children should become slaves." Mohammed, pleased with the verdict, said, "You have made a ruling that Allah or a king would approve of."

The Jewish men were made to dig their own graves. Mohammed and his 12 year old bride then sat and watched all day and into the night, while 800 of them were beheaded. Any boy who did not have pubic hair was saved and raised as a Muslim.

The spoils were then divided up, with Mohammed taking his usual twenty percent. The rest was divided up amongst his warriors. The women were taken to a nearby town, where they were sold as sex slaves. The one exception was the most beautiful Jewess, who Mohammed took to use himself. He had killed her husband and all of her male relatives, and now used her for his own pleasure.

The Koran makes mention of this event:
33:26 He brought down some of the People of the Book [the Jews] out of their fortresses to aid the confederates and to strike terror into their hearts. Some you killed, and others you took captive. He made you heirs of their land, their homes, and their possessions, and even gave you another land on which you had never before set foot. Allah has power over everything.

Author's Comments:
I'm not often at a loss for words, but I can't think what to say about this event. People who haven't read these books often tell me that their meaning depends upon how you interpret them, so I'll leave you to decide how to interpret this event. Here is a question you might want to ponder. Why are "radical" Muslims so keen on cutting people's heads off? The Saudi's will do it for such heinous crimes as disagreeing with Mohammed, or deciding to change your religion. Jihadists delight in beheading Kaffirs, (even aid workers) and posting the video on the internet. Now you know whose example they are following.

To a Christian, Jesus never did anything wrong. He didn't lie, cheat, steal, kill, swear, etc. in fact he was perfect. What most people don't realize is that the reason he never misbehaved, is because our concept of right and wrong is based upon the example of his life. If Jesus had lived a different kind of life, then Christian based societies would have a different concept of what constituted right and wrong, or good and evil.

There are examples throughout history of people who claimed to be Christians, committing acts of brutality on a par with Mohammed. This does not affect what Christianity is, because Christianity is not based on the example of such people; it is based on the example of Jesus as recorded in the Gospels. Likewise Islam is not based on the example of just any old Muslim; it is based on the example of Mohammed as recorded in *The Sira* and the hadith. Islam holds Mohammed to be the perfect man and the perfect example for Muslims to follow for all time.

Slavery

Mohammed had always approved of slavery. One of his first converts was a slave who he owned. Whenever he took captives, if they weren't ransomed or killed, they would be sold into slavery. Women especially, were valued for their use as sex slaves. Mohammed owned many slaves. He bought them, sold them and took them captive. His son was born to one of his slaves, a Christian girl named Mary.[13] Throughout Islamic history, slavery has therefore been not only acceptable, but desirable, as it advanced Islam. Its abolition was forced after the conquest of Islamic lands by Christian nations, particularly Great Britain and the United States. Slavery was finally officially abolished in Saudi Arabia in 1962 under pressure from the West. It is still thought to exist unofficially in some Muslim countries.

Sub Saharan Africa was a major source of slaves for the Muslims. After Barak Obama won the US Presidency, the press reported that Al Qaeda considered him to be like a "House Slave" or "House Negro."[14] In Arabic, the word "Abd" means a slave. The name "Abdullah" means the slave of Allah. The word "Abd" also means Negro.

---

[13] He died before reaching adulthood

[14] http://www.theguardian.com/world/2008/nov/19/alqaida-zawahiri-obama-white-house

15 An Attempted Assassination

After the Battle of the trench Mohammed sent assassins to kill his chief rival in Mecca, Abu Sufyan.

From the Biography by Al-Tabari:[15]
T1438 Mohammed sent two men to Mecca to kill his rival, Abu Sufyan. The plan was simple and the leader was from Mecca so he knew it well. They set out on one camel for Abu Sufyan's home where one man would stand watch and the other would go in and put a knife in him. But the assisting Muslim wanted to go to the Kabah and pray. The leader argued against it because he was well known, but the other Muslim insisted. So they went to the Kabah and sure enough, the leader was recognized. The Meccans set up a cry of alarm and the men fled Mecca. There was no way to kill Abu Sufyan now.
T1439 The Muslims ran to a cave on the outskirts of Mecca. They placed rocks in front of the cave and waited quietly. A Meccan approached the cave while cutting grass for his horse. The Muslim leader came out of the cave and killed him with a knife thrust to the belly. The man screamed loudly, and his companions came running; however, they were more concerned with their dying comrade than the killers and left carrying the body. The Muslims waited for a while and then fled again.
T1440 On their way back to Medina, the Muslims met a one-eyed shepherd. It turned out that they were related by clan ties. The shepherd said he was not a Muslim nor would he ever be. As they sat talking, the shepherd lay back and went to sleep. The leader took his bow and drove its tip down through the shepherd's one eye, into his

---

[15] The original manuscript of Ibn Ishaq's biography was lost in the very early days. *The Sira* was therefore reconstructed from the notes and writings of two of his students, Ibn Hashim and Al-Tabari. This section is therefore taken from *"The Sira"*

brain, and out the back of his head. Then they headed on back to Medina.

T1440 On the road, the leader saw two Meccans who were enemies of Islam. He shot one and captured the other and marched him to Medina. When they got to Mohammed with the captive and told him the whole story of the killing, Mohammed laughed so hard they could see his back teeth. Then he blessed them.

Author's Comments:

In his early days as a prophet in Mecca, Mohammed had not been violent at all. His teachings were religious and confined to threats in the afterlife. By this stage however, his hatred of those who refused to believe in him could be described as inhuman. His personality is described by psychiatrists as narcissistic. He demanded adoration from others and showed a psychopathic hatred of those who would not give him the status he demanded. At its core, these are the values on which Islam is founded.

Muslims believe that there is no God but Allah and Mohammed is his final Prophet. Mohammed is believed to be perfect and the Koran tells Muslims repeatedly to emulate his behaviour. As we already know, Muslims can choose to follow Mohammed's Meccan example, as most of them do or follow the Medina example as the Jihadists do. Since earlier verses are abrogated by later ones, the Medinan Koran is better, but since the Koran is perfect the Meccan Koran is also valid.

To a Western mind this is very confusing. By our logic, if two things contradict each other then at least one must be wrong. Western logic is founded on truth and only one thing can be true. In Islamic logic, "truth" is anything which advances Islam. Two things therefore can contradict one another and yet both are "true".

The confusion this causes is deliberate and Islam often uses it to its own advantage. Its hard (Medinan) side hides behind its softer (Meccan) side. This is one reason why "moderate" Muslims may complain about Jihadists to Kaffirs, but will never confront the Jihadists themselves. They know that the Medina example is the better one.

16 Jihad Continues

Mohammed was now head of an extremely powerful political force. He began attacking and conquering other tribes around Medina. They were given a choice. They could convert to Islam, or else be killed and their women taken for slaves of pleasure. Because of his power he was beginning to attract even more followers. Some were attracted to the war booty, some wanted to be on the winning side and others were afraid that they would be next.

Bukhari's Hadith records one of the problems that Mohammed's men were having at this time with the female captives and Mohammed's response.

B5,59,459 Entering the mosque, Ibn Muhairiz saw Abu Said and asked him whether coitus interruptus was sanctified by Allah. Abu Said said, "Accompanying Mohammed at the Battle of Banu Al-Mustaliq, we were rewarded with Arab captives, including several woman which were very sought after because celibacy had become quite a hardship. We had planned to practice coitus interruptus but felt that we should seek instruction first from Mohammed. [Ed. Pregnancy was undesirable in the slaves because it diminished their value on the market.] Mohammed said, however, 'It is better that you not interrupt copulation to prevent pregnancy, because if a soul is predestined to exist, then it will exist.'"

The interesting point here (apart from the obvious inhumanity of endorsing the taking and subsequent rape of slaves) is Mohammed's insistence on predestination. Muslims often use the phrase "inshallah" which translates as "God (Allah) willing." In other words nothing will happen unless Allah has already planned it. This might not seem like a big deal, but in fact it has a huge impact on Islamic societies. Since

Muslims believe that they will not be killed unless Allah wills it, there is no point worrying about being killed. This makes Muslims immensely brave in battle compared to non-Muslims. The downside is that it also makes them extremely lazy and unproductive in peace time. Muslims believe that nothing will improve unless Allah wills it. Why then would they struggle to improve things? This becomes the ultimate excuse in Islamic societies. "Why didn't you do the job I gave you?"

"Well obviously Allah didn't want me to!"

"Why didn't you show up for work last week?"

"Well Allah just willed it that way."

Mohammed had no interest in his followers producing anything; he was solely interested in conquest. He financed his society from war booty. Every part of Islamic culture is moulded to serve this end.

When academics examine backwardness and poverty in Islamic countries today, it is fashionable to blame it on the aggression and exploitation of the West. These problems however, are almost universal in Islamic countries. Surely then, we should be analysing the impact of Islamic teachings on human progress in these societies.

The Treaty of al Hudaybiya

Mohammed decided to make a pilgrimage to Mecca. The Meccans would not let him enter the city however, even though he came without the intention of making war.

From *The Sira*:

1747 The Meccans sent a man out to make a treaty with Mohammed. Umar was furious that Mohammed would make a treaty with non-Muslims because it was demeaning to Islam. But Mohammed told him Allah would not let them lose; they would win over the Quraysh. Be patient.

So they drew up a treaty to the effect that there would be no war for ten years. There would be no hostilities and no child could convert to Islam without a guardian's permission. In return, the Muslims could come the following year and stay for three days in Mecca though they could not enter that year.

When Mohammed made peace, it was never for the sake of peace. It was always a strategic decision to wait until he could build up his strength. Patience was one of his greatest strengths in his quest to conquer the world. It remains the cornerstone of Islamic strategy today. Compare this with Hitler's tactics. He blundered into Russia whilst simultaneously trying to conquer Great Britain, almost losing his entire army along the way. Mohammed would only bite off as much as he could chew. He wouldn't move on until he had digested it.

17 Khaybar, the First Dhimmis

Two months after the treaty of Hudaybiya, Mohammed marched his army 100 miles to Khaybar, to attack a community of Jews who lived there. Mohammed never had any problems with the Jews of Khaybar. His raid was motivated purely by greed. The Jews of Khaybar were wealthy farmers who lived in a series of forts amongst their crops.

From *The Sira*:
I757 When Mohammed raided a people, he waited until the morning. If he heard the call to prayer, which meant the people were Muslims, he would not attack but if there was no Muslim call to prayer he attacked. When he rode up with his army, workers were coming out to work in the fields. When they saw Mohammed and his army, they fled. Mohammed said, "Allah Akbar! Khaybar is destroyed. When we arrive in a people's Square, it is a bad morning for those who have been warned."

Mohammed was now one of the most powerful men in Arabia thanks to Jihad. Unlike in the early days, he could now do pretty much as he pleased. He set about destroying all opposition, showing absolutely no mercy to any who resisted him.

I758 Mohammed seized the forts one at a time. Among the captives was a beautiful Jewess named Safiyah. Mohammed took her for his sexual pleasure. One of his men had first chosen her for his own slave of pleasure, but Mohammed traded him two of her cousins for Safiyah. Mohammed always got first choice of the spoils of war and the women.
I759 On the occasion of Khaybar, Mohammed put forth new orders about forcing sex with captive women. If the woman was pregnant, she was not to be used for sex until after the birth of the child. Nor were

56

any women to be used for sex who were unclean with regard to Muslim laws about menstruation.

1764 Mohammed knew there was a large treasure hidden somewhere in Khaybar so he brought forth the Jew he thought knew the most about it and questioned him. This Jew was Kinana, the husband of Safiyah, Mohammed's soon-to-be new bride. Kinana denied any knowledge. But another Jew said he had seen the man around one of the old ruins. The search was made, and a great deal of the treasure was found but not all of it. Mohammed told one of his men, "Torture the Jew until you extract what he has." So the Jew was staked on the ground and a small fire built on his chest to get him to talk. The man was nearly dead but would not talk, so Mohammed had him released and taken to one of his men whose brother had been killed in the fight, and the Muslim got the pleasure of cutting the tortured Jew's head off.

Muslims believe that Mohammed was the perfect man and the Koran repeatedly tells Muslims to emulate his behaviour. Most Muslims have never read his biographies and rely on Imams for guidance. In times or places where Islam is weak, we would expect these Imams to counsel people to follow Mohammed's Meccan example. History shows however, that when Islam becomes powerful, things change.

From *The Sira*:
1764 The Jews of Khaybar were Mohammed's first dhimmis. After the best of the goods were taken from the Jews, Mohammed left them to work the land. His men knew nothing about farming and the Jews were skilled at it. So the Jews worked the land and gave Mohammed half their profits.

Author's Comments:
This was a new tactic which would become an important part of the overall strategy of Islam. Up until this point Kaffirs were given two choices; convert to Islam or be killed. Now, a third option was introduced, dhimmitude. A dhimmi is a non-Muslim living in a land ruled by Islam. They are forced to pay a poll tax (Jizya) to the Muslims, which can be as high as 50% of their income. Most importantly, they must also be made to feel humiliated. They have few rights and are allowed to follow their religion in private. They must not however, repair or replace their churches or synagogues (dhimmitude is only supposed to be available to Jews and Christians).

With Islam being so geared towards conquest, its societies lack productive capacity. By allowing the Christians and Jews to live in semi slavery, Islam now had a source of income even in peace time. The institution of Dhimmitude was developed further under the later caliphs, and is an important part of the system of Jihad.

The Koran spoke about Dhimmitude:

9:29 Make war on those who have received the scriptures (Jews and Christians) but do not believe in Allah or in the last day. They do not forbid what Allah and his messenger have forbidden. The Christians and Jews do not follow the religion of truth until they submit and pay the poll tax (Jizya), and they are humiliated.

We are often told that Jews and Christians were allowed to live in peace and harmony in Muslim lands. To someone who does not understand the onerous conditions of dhimmitude, this would suggest an inherent tolerance in Islam which does not exist.

From *The Sira*:

1766 On the way back Mohammed had one of the Muslim women Prepare Safiyah (she was the Jewess he had picked for his pleasure) for her wedding night with Mohammed. That night one of his men marched around his tent for the whole night with his sword. The next morning Mohammed asked what he was doing and the man replied, "I was afraid for you because of the woman. You have killed her father, her husband, and her kin, so I was afraid for you on her account." Mohammed blessed him.

The phrase "Allahu Akbar" has become infamous, especially since the 9/11 attacks. The hijacker's leader, Mohammed Atta, had spent the previous night touring strip clubs. As they flew their jets into the Twin Towers, slaughtering Kaffirs the attackers were recorded yelling "Allahu Akbar". This is usually translated as "Allah is great", but actually means "Allah is greater" (as in, "greater than all other gods").

This phrase is not a modern Jihadist invention. It is the battle cry of the very first Jihadist, the Prophet Mohammed, as he slaughtered innocent Kaffirs.

After the 9/11 attacks, George Bush and UK Prime Minister Tony Blair (and all other world leaders to this day) declared that these attacks had nothing to do with Islam. Since that time, the words Jihad, Islamist, Muslim, Islam and all reference to Islamic Doctrine have been purged from US anti-terror manuals. To understand the reason for this type of reaction, it is important to know more about dhimmitude.

18 More About Dhimmitude

The institution of Dhimmitude was a unique Islamic development, which created a special class of citizens. These people were allowed to exist in a subservient status. They were conquered people in their own lands under Islamic domination. This situation existed across the Islamic world, until it was conquered by the Western (Christian) nations. Unfortunately Dhimmitude is not just an institution; it is a submissive mindset adopted by victims of bullying and intimidation everywhere. Successful bullies instinctively understand the importance of inflicting this mindset on their victims. By doing so, they can gain total control with a minimum of effort.

Many of us have witnessed the tragedy of women who have been physically and psychologically abused by husbands for years. Often they defend the actions of the abuser whilst blaming themselves for the abuse ("If only I hadn't served dinner too late he would never have beaten me").

Tyrants instinctively understand this method of oppression. That is why it is so hard for subjected people to overthrow them. By building this method into his doctrine, Mohammed ensured that once conquered by Islam, no revolt by dhimmis would ever be possible. In fact no society which has been conquered by Islam has ever freed itself without outside help.

Let me repeat that:
Historically, NO SOCIETY WHICH HAS BEEN CONQUERED BY ISLAM HAS EVER FREED ITSELF WITHOUT OUTSIDE HELP.

M. Lal Goel (A Hindu) Professor Emeritus of Political Science [16]
writes of the Islamic institution of Dhimmitude:

Dhimmitude is a state of fear and insecurity on the part of infidels who are required to accept a condition of humiliation. It is characterized by the victim's siding with his oppressors, by the moral justification the victim provides for his oppressors' hateful behaviour. The Dhimmi loses the possibility of revolt because revolt arises from a sense of injustice. He loathes himself in order to praise his oppressors. Dhimmis lived under some 20 disabilities. Dhimmis were prohibited to build new places of worship, to ring church bells or take out processions, to ride horses or camels (they could ride donkeys), to marry a Muslim woman, to wear decorative clothing, to own a Muslim as a slave or to testify against a Muslim in a court of law.

After WW1 when the Ottoman (Turkish) Empire was defeated, the institution of dhimmitude was supposed to have been abolished. Unfortunately, this phenomenon continues as a state of mind. It is growing almost daily around the world, as people submit spiritually and emotionally to Islamic superiority.

For example, in 2006, the Pope gave his famous Regensburg address. In it he quoted a Byzantine emperor, who said that Islam had never brought forth anything into this world except violence. The Pope did not endorse this view. He merely used it as an example to make a theological point in a somewhat abstract discussion.

Muslims around the world immediately began to protest. In England, church goers were harassed by Muslim protesters, but elsewhere things were far worse. Attacks by Muslims against Christians escalated and in Somalia, a nun who was doing humanitarian work, (for Muslims) was shot in the back. What was the Pope's reaction? We would not of course expect him to be undiplomatic and declare "I told you Islam is violent." He could however have kept his peace, as traditionally the Pope never apologizes. Instead, he chose to act as a dhimmi and apologize to the Muslims.

By apologizing, he sent a message to the world that his statements had caused the violence, not the raging Muslims who carried it out. Once the Pope apologized, the Muslims stopped rioting. Islam had achieved its goal. The Pope had recognized that he had wronged Islam and caused the violence against Christians, he would never do this again.

---

[16]www.uwf.edu/lgoel

61

This is how Jihad works, slowly, step by step, leaders, opinion makers, academics, journalists, organizations and eventually the general population, are cowed into submission, (remember, Islam is Arabic for submission) and forced to accept responsibility for deliberate Islamic attacks against them.

Pretty soon, people get the message and every attack is greeted with the expected response, "what must we have done to cause this, it must be our fault because of the invasion of Iraq/Afghanistan/support for Israel/the Crusades/discrimination/islamophobia/our causing poverty etc. etc."

Never ever, does Islam take responsibility because it is a peaceful religion with a few (million?) extremists who have misunderstood it.

Now imagine yourself in the position of a military commander trying to take control of a nation. Every time you attack your intended victim, they blame themselves for your aggression. They hold inquiries to find which of them is guilty. Instead of attacking you, they attack their own Government/institutions/anyone they can think of. How can you lose? Just keep up a relentless series of attacks and blame the victim every time until finally, they capitulate.

Now can you understand the awesome power of Jihad? You can't beat it with nuclear weapons, smart bombs, or stealth bombers. It doesn't matter how many laser guided missiles or unmanned drones you have. It doesn't matter how well trained your army is. If you are too afraid to admit who your enemy is, then you might as well throw them all in the bin for the good they will do you. You cannot beat Jihad with force, it is too powerful; don't even bother thinking about it, the army will not save you from Jihad.

The only thing that will save us from Jihad is the truth and:

Truth cannot exist without courage.

19 Dhimmitude Today

The importance of the psychological aspect of dhimmitude and how it affects our society today, cannot be stressed enough. The idea of dhimmitude may be difficult for people to process however. I wanted therefore to give some more examples to illustrate the presence of dhimmitude in our society.

Since the early Sixties, the feminist movement has been extremely vocal in advocating women's rights. They launched a huge and successful campaign, for equal pay and rights for women at work. They even became passionate over inconsequential issues such as a woman's right to work on a nuclear submarine (locked in a tin can with 400 men for months on end). Why then do they ignore Islamic anti-women issues such as female genital mutilation, honour killings, women being stoned to death for adultery etc? Why does the feminist movement keep a disciplined silence when confronted by Islamic violence to women? The conclusion, feminists have mostly become dhimmis.

The United Kingdom is ostensibly a Christian nation, yet today it is becoming ever less acceptable to celebrate Christmas in public. Councils are refusing to put up Christmas trees and shops are now selling cards saying things like "Winter Wishes." Even the Red Cross (which was founded by a devout Christian) now refuses to display Nativity scenes in their windows. Apparently the festival of "peace on earth and goodwill to all men," might be offensive to people of "other" religions.

The BBC now avoids using the terms AD (Year of our Lord) or BC (Before Christ) when quoting dates, as these are derived from Christianity. They instead use the terms CE (Common Era) or BCE (Before Common Era). They are however happy to announce times and dates for Islamic holidays.

These are just a few of the examples of the creeping dhimmitude in our societies, of which there are thousands; but where do these things come from? Is political correctness just a spontaneous occurrence or is it being driven by Islam. If so how could they be achieving this? Is this the hallmark of a stealth takeover of our society by Islam?

These are important questions and we will examine a few of the ways in which Islam could (and I suspect does) influence the institutions of Western societies to facilitate this gradual Islamization. This is a little UK centric although the same trends are in place all over the Western World.

Influencing the Government:
Cash
When the Global Financial crisis hit in 2008 the finances of the UK's banking system were in tatters. Then Prime Minister Gordon Brown panicked and jumped on a plane, presumably to secure cash from his closest allies. Rather than heading for Washington, Brussels or Paris however, he went straight to Riyadh (Saudi Arabia). [17] The question is, why would the Saudi's be willing to provide enough cash to rescue a banking system the size of Britain's? Even more importantly, what would they be expecting in return? (News Flash: there is no such thing as a free lunch). The GFC was a complete surprise to British politicians. This suggests that it wasn't the first time the British Government had received Saudi cash (or promises thereof).

We all know how harmful cigarettes are and yet for years, governments have resisted calls to restrict their use. I don't think any sensible person would think that this has nothing to do with the cash which tobacco companies have lavished on politicians of all stripes.

If a tobacco company can buy favours from a democratic government, imagine how much more influence an entire nation could have. This would be especially true if it happened to be rich with oil wealth.

It would be easy to achieve this influence, even without direct funding. By offering such incentives as preferential contracts to oil companies and weapons suppliers etc. it would be possible to exert considerable influence on democratic governments. It would be particularly effective if these companies were large political donors in their own right.

---

[17] http://news.bbc.co.uk/2/hi/uk_news/politics/7704627.stm

For example, in the mid 1980's, an arms deal between Saudi Arabia and the UK was touted as, "the biggest [UK] sale ever of anything to anyone", "staggering both by its sheer size and complexity". Hundreds of millions of pounds were reputed to have been paid in "commissions" alone. Margaret Thatcher's son was reported to have received twelve million pounds himself. [18]

The UK National Audit Office investigated the deal, but its findings were withheld. Apparently, this was "the only NAO report ever to be withheld". [19]

An investigation by the UK's Serious Fraud Office was also subsequently dropped, after political pressure from Prime Minister Tony Blair. He was concerned to prevent embarrassment to the Saudis which might endanger future arms sales.

The British Government was prepared to bend over backwards and ride roughshod over its own legal processes to secure this money. What other concessions might they have been prepared to make?

Votes

As well as finance, Islam now controls a sizeable voting bloc in the UK, with Muslims now making up more than 3% of the population. With most elections going to the wire these days, a 52% majority is considered to be a landslide. With a high degree of control exercised by the Mosque over the lives of Muslims, this gives Islam a huge degree of leverage over the government. Tony Blair found this out to his cost when he invaded Iraq/Afghanistan. Whatever your thoughts on the rights or wrongs of this particular incident, the fact remains that Britain's foreign policy is now being influenced by Islam.

Terror

In November 2007, MI5 announced that it was monitoring around 2000 Islamic terror plots in the UK. Presumably there must be a few they don't know about. Any time the British Government makes a decision which impacts unfavourably on Muslims, they are reminded sternly of the possible retaliation by "extreme elements." No

---

[18]http://www.independent.co.uk/news/uk/the-mark-thatcher-affair-arms-deal-triumph-for-batting-for-britain-steve-boggan-examines-the-history-of-the-biggest-weapons-agreement-ever-struck-between-two-countries-1441987.html

[19]http://en.wikipedia.org/wiki/Al-Yamamah_arms_deal#Investigation_discontinued

Government wants to be held responsible for aggravating such an attack.

Assassination
In Holland, Geert Wilders runs a political party which opposes Islamic encroachment, for all the reasons I have outlined in this book. He lives under 24/7 protection and will for the rest of his life. Few politicians display such courage.

Meanwhile, Back in Arabia....
Mohammed's behaviour was beginning to have the desired effect on other tribes nearby:

From *The Sira*:
1777 The Jews of Fadak panicked when they saw what Mohammed did to Khaybar. They would be next, so they surrendered to Mohammed without a fight. Since there was no battle Mohammed got 100 percent of their goods, and they worked the land and gave half to Mohammed each year. They became dhimmis like those of Khaybar.

Author's Comments:
Islam operates through intimidation. It gains power over people by making them afraid. Once it dominates by fear, it makes demands. These invariably involve a society giving up the ability to defend itself, in return for being allowed to live peacefully. These demands are usually made incrementally, especially at first and are framed as reasonably as possible. Recent examples were Islamic demands that they not be profiled at airports, or searched by dogs. This despite the fact that most threats to aircraft have come from Islamic groups.

Having capitulated to this demand, governments are then even more vulnerable to terror attacks on planes. This makes them more likely to agree to the next demand, such as the silencing of free speech, further weakening the society's defences.

As this cycle continues, the Kaffirs become ever weaker while Islam becomes stronger and stronger. The eventual aim, according to a number of the more extreme Islamic groups, is the establishment of Sharia Law, which institutionalizes the Kaffirs as second class citizens, or "dhimmis."

66

20 War Treasure

1770 A Meccan named Al Hajjaj became a Muslim and took part in the capture of Khaybar. After the conquest he asked Mohammed's permission to go to Mecca and finish up his affairs and collect his debts. He then asked Mohammed if he could tell lies to get his money. The prophet of Allah said, "Tell them." So he set out for Mecca. When he got there the Meccans were asking for news from Khaybar. They did not know that the man had converted and so trusted him. He told them the Muslims had lost and that Mohammed had been captured. He said the Jews of Khaybar were going to bring Mohammed to Mecca so they could kill him.

1771 The Meccans were elated. He then asked them to help him collect his debts so he could return to Khaybar and profit from the confusion there. In good spirits they helped him collect the debts. He had been gone three days when they found out the truth of Khaybar and the fact that he was now a Muslim.

Author's Comments:

Once again we see the example of Mohammed, allowing his followers to deceive Kaffirs to gain advantage over them. This was one of his favourite tactics and is described repeatedly in his biographies. To this day it remains a central pillar of Jihad and even has a name. In Arabic it is known as Taquiya, or sacred deceit.

1774 There were a total of eighteen hundred people who divided up the wealth taken from the Jews of Khaybar. A cavalry man got three shares; a foot soldier got one share. Mohammed appointed eighteen chiefs to divide the loot. Mohammed got his fifth before it was distributed.

Mohammed was not interested in an opulent lifestyle. Even his wives complained of the lowly conditions they lived in whilst he was so wealthy. His main motivation seems to have been his desire to be worshipped by all. Most of his wealth was spent on weapons and supplies for Jihad, or in the payment of monies to settle disputes amongst his followers (blood money). In the later part of his life, Mohammed's all consuming passion was the conquest of the Kaffirs. It is also a major component of the religion he created.

In the previous chapter we looked at the influence of Islam on Western Governments, in this one we will look at how it influences another institution.

Islamic Influence in Universities

Most universities are run by Governments. Islam therefore has a means to influence them through its degree of control over government decisions. Wealthy Muslims also donate huge sums of money to universities around the Western world, giving them the potential to influence decisions and policies. Leaders in most fields pass through university. The information which is disseminated in them is therefore of great importance for the future of our societies.

In March 2008, Alwaleed Bin Talal had donated £8m to build an Islamic studies centre (to bear his name) at Cambridge University. A few months later, on 8 May 2008, he gave £ 16m to Edinburgh University to fund the "centre for the study of Islam in the contemporary world." In April 2009, Al Waleed donated $20 million to Harvard University, one of its 25 largest donations. He also donated the same amount to Georgetown University.

His donation and others coming from Islamic sources have not been always welcomed due to their effects on academic objectivity and security concerns.[20]

Muslims are obliged to give to a percentage of their income to charity; however money given to Kaffirs does not count. When six out of ten Muslims worldwide are illiterate[21], it seems strange that Muslims are pouring such huge sums of money into Western universities. It is hard to imagine that such generosity doesn't come with conditions. Perhaps this is why universities are so reluctant to

---

[20] http://en.wikipedia.org/wiki/Al-Waleed_bin_Talal

[21]http://www.webcitation.org/query?url=http://web.archive.org/web/20051129011120/http://www.jang.com.pk/thenews/nov2005-daily/08-11-2005/oped/o6.htm&date=2012-08-14

criticize Islam. Instead, they produce documents roundly endorsing Islam. These offer sanitized, airbrushed accounts of Islamic history and achievements which bear little resemblance to the truth[22].

This may also be why Middle Eastern studies courses never examine Islamic Doctrine or Jihad. This seems strange given the undeniably huge influence that Islam has on the Middle East. In fact, Islamic Doctrine is not studied in any Western university period. Whether this influence extends beyond Middle Eastern studies, into broader history and social studies generally is hard to know. Circumstantial evidence suggests however, that it does.

For instance, we all learn about Africans being taken to America as slaves by Europeans. Why then do we not learn about the Barbary (North African Muslim) Pirates? For centuries, they raided shipping and coastal villages around Europe. They reached as far as the UK and took more than a million Europeans back to sell as slaves in North Africa and the Middle East[23]. Huge swathes of European coastline had to be abandoned for fear of these African slavers. Their trade was finally stopped in 1830 when the French invaded Algeria.

(By comparison, detailed shipping records exist, showing a total of 388,000 African slaves were shipped to the USA prior to 1798 when the trade was voluntarily abolished).[24]

How many people today are aware of the constant attacks which for centuries were launched against Eastern Europe by the Ottoman Turks? They took so many European slaves back to the Middle East that the word "Slave" is derived from the word "Slav."

Why do we not learn of the 1400 years of Islamic slave trading in Africa, but only of the 200 years of European slave trading?

There is no reason not to examine the many instances of wrong doing by Western societies in the past. It is in fact one of the great strengths of Western society, that we can admit to and learn from our mistakes. To pretend however that Europeans were the only wrong doers in the entire world's history and that all current problems can be traced to past evils of Western/Christian nations, seems suspiciously like the attitude of a dhimmi. Whether these two pieces of information (Islamic financing of universities and academic self-blame) are

---

[22] For example: Learning from One Another: Bringing Muslim perspectives into Australian schools by Hassim and Cole-Adams
National Centre of Excellence for Islamic Studies, University of Melbourne
http://www.nceis.unimelb.edu.au

[23] http://researchnews.osu.edu/archive/whtslav.htm

[24] http://www.slavevoyages.org/tast/assessment/estimates.faces

connected or not is hard to say, but they seem to fit pretty neatly in with the rest of the jigsaw. At the very least, it seems remarkable that the UK could be at war with Muslims in two different Islamic countries, (Iraq/Afghanistan) and yet the only study of the enemy's doctrine/philosophy/motivation is being conducted by Muslims. Some call this political correctness, in the long term it sounds more like political suicide.

From "The Australian" Newspaper Letters Page, September 19, 2012

Your editorial calls for an open, frank and ongoing discussion in the battle of ideas about contemporary Islam. Tragically, such open discussion is not possible in our universities, as I have discovered to my cost.

My refusal to adopt a pro-Islamist terrorist and anti-American position in the aftermath of the 9/11 attacks led to a concerted campaign of vilification against me that lasted for several years and only subsided when I won a Work Cover case against my employer.

Moreover, over the past decade there have been many demands that I be sacked for publishing my views on Islamist extremism and I have also been threatened several times with legal action. One of the persons who made such threats - and also demanded my dismissal - is a senior academic who teaches at Australia's premier defence academy. Another holds a leadership position in a national centre of excellence in Islamic studies.

Unfortunately, this prolonged series of attacks on me for engaging in public debate about Islam and Islamist extremism has seriously damaged my health and has now led to my early retirement. Such is the price of academic discussion of Islam in this country.

Mervyn F. Bendle, Townsville, Qld

21 The Death of a Poetess

*1996 There was a poetess who wrote a poem against Islam.
Mohammed said, "Who will rid me of Marwan's daughter?" One of
his followers heard him and on that very night he went to the woman's
home to kill her.*

*M239 The assassin, a blind man, was able to do the work in the dark
as the woman slept. Her babe lay on her breast while her other
children slept in the room. The stealthy assassin removed the child
and drove the knife into her with such force that he pinned her to the
bed.*

*1996 In the morning he went to Mohammed and told him. Mohammed
said, "You have helped Allah and his apostle." When asked about the
consequences, Mohammed said, "Two goats won't butt their heads
together over this."*

*M239 Mohammed turned to the people in the mosque and said, "If
you wish to see a man who has assisted Allah and his prophet, look
here." Omar cried, "What, the blind Omeir!" "No," said Mohammed,
"call him Omeir the Seeing."*

*1996 The mother, had five sons and the assassin went to the sons and
said, "I killed Bint Marwan [The daughter of Marwan], O sons.
Withstand me if you can; don't keep me waiting." Islam became
powerful that day and many became Muslims when they saw the
power of Islam.*

Author's Comments:

Marwan's daughter was angry that some of her tribe's chiefs had
been murdered. These murders had been committed by Muslims with
Mohammed's approval. Her tribe was not prepared to fight
Mohammed for retribution and so she composed a poem critical of
him. In a desert world with virtually no written material available, a

71

poem was like a newspaper article which would be told and passed around by word of mouth. Naturally, Mohammed soon came to hear of it.

Mohammed knew that this woman posed no threat to him. Her tribe had already made it abundantly clear that they would not attack the Muslims but this was not enough for Mohammed. Like bullies and tyrants everywhere, Mohammed knew that the key to absolute control of a group is the destruction of free speech.

When people are afraid to criticize an oppressor, the whole group dynamic changes. Silence becomes a form of tacit approval and nobody knows who is a supporter and who is an opponent. Defiance then becomes almost impossible. People find themselves isolated from those of similar persuasion and individuals who do speak out are easily picked off. As this process intensifies, fear builds and the tyrants grip on society tightens. This process is referred to as "consolidation of power".

The polar opposite to this situation is a society in which free speech is protected, because:

Tyranny and free speech cannot coexist in a society.

In order to protect free speech, it is not enough to protect most speech; you have to protect all speech. Once the ruling classes have the right to restrict speech deemed unpleasant, they will invariably restrict opposition to themselves. When this is achieved, freedom is lost forever.

There are of course some well understood exceptions to this principle. Yelling fire in a crowded theatre, inciting people to violence or harming people and their reputation with lies are examples of speech which is not protected. Insulting, ridiculing, upsetting or humiliating people (or their ideas) *is* protected in a free society. In fact the ability to do this, is the very definition of a free society.

It is important to understand that free speech is not the right to tell people what they want to hear. Free speech is the right to tell people what they *do not* want to hear. No one in Saddam Hussein's Iraq was ever imprisoned for saying what a great guy Saddam was, despite the fact that free speech was not a right for Iraqis. This is the point about free speech, it is not the ability to say "most" things, It is the ability to say absolutely anything (outside of the exceptions noted above) without fear of retribution.

The "problem" with free speech, is that people will invariably say things which *you* don't like. Some people will say that the holocaust never happened or that heroin or slavery should be legalized. Unfortunately, if you want to have free speech, this is what comes with it.

Votaire realized the importance of this when he declared, "I may not agree with what you say, but I will fight to the death for your right to say it."

No matter how much you want to stop people from denying the holocaust or advocating rights for child molesters, you cannot do this without destroying freedom of speech.

The important thing to note, is that if you don't like an idea, you have the right to argue against it. If the idea really is bad, then that should be easy.

The notion of Islam as a peaceful and decent religion seems pretty difficult to defend in reasoned argument. Mohammed, like tyrants everywhere understood that the only way to win this argument was through violence, threats and intimidation.

This then is the final tactic of Jihad:

Rules of Jihad:
8) Never ever allow criticism of Mohammed, Allah or Islam, destroy free speech.

22 Free Speech Today

Free speech is a bedrock principle of free societies everywhere. It is no coincidence that nations which have historically protected free speech are nations such as the UK, USA, most of Western Europe, Canada, Australia, etc. Those which restrict free speech include the likes of Burma, North Korea, China, Russia and all of the Islamic countries including Iran, Iraq, Somalia, Pakistan, etc.

Western nations have protected free speech since before most of us were born. Most people seem to think that they always will. These people haven't been paying attention, so please sit up because this is where things start to get scary.

57 majority Islamic Nations form an organization called the Organization of Islamic Cooperation or OIC. This is the largest voting bloc in the United Nations and for years it has been working to persuade UN member countries to ban criticism of religions (specifically Islam). Recently these efforts seem to have been bearing fruit.

When I grew up, people understood that you couldn't call the police just because someone offended you. In fact, it was considered childish to be overly concerned with insults.

In recent years however, a combination of Multiculturalism and Political Correctness has been steadily eroding this freedom. Today, people who speak out against Islam are likely to find themselves in court, fighting for their freedom, or even in jail.

In Denmark, the president of the "Danish Free Press Society", Lars Hedegaard was forced to appeal a conviction for "Hate Speech".

Here are some highlights from an article posted at the Gatestone Institute[25] (emphasis mine)

---

[25] http://www.gatestoneinstitute.org/3011/hate-speech-charges

Editor's note: On April 13[2012], Lars Hedegaard, President of the Danish Free Press Society, appealed to Denmark's Supreme Court to overturn his conviction by Denmark's Superior Court on May 3, 2011, after two years in lower courts, on charges of alleged Hate Speech. Under Denmark's Article 266(b), **it is immaterial if what one says is true; evidence in support of the truth is inadmissible.** *All that matters is if someone has said something in public that might cause someone to "feel offended,"* **or if the prosecutor thinks someone might be justified in "feeling offended.**" *After Mr. Hedegaard spoke privately about the Muslim treatment of women, a tape of his remarks was disseminated, apparently without his knowledge or approval. The accuracy of what he said was not in dispute. A verdict is expected this week.*

The following is an edited transcript of his courtroom defence:

If our Western freedom means anything at all, we must insist that every grown-up person is responsible for his or her beliefs, opinions, culture, habits and actions.

We enjoy political freedom and we enjoy freedom of religion. This implies a largely unlimited right to disseminate one's political persuasion and religious beliefs. That is as it should be. But the price we all have to pay for this freedom is that others have a right to criticise our politics, our religion and our culture.

Islamic spokesmen have the freedom to advocate their concept of society, which implies the introduction of a theocracy governed by God-given laws, i.e. Sharia, the abolition of man-made laws and by implication freedom of expression and democracy. They are free to think that women are inferior to men as concerns their rights and their pursuit of happiness. They are even entitled to disseminate such opinions.

I cannot recall a single instance in this country where an Islamic spokesman has been prosecuted for saying that, of course, Sharia will become the law of the land once the demographic and political realities make it possible. This despite the fact that we have several examples of, e.g., imams who have openly declared that the imposition of theocracy is a religious duty incumbent on all believers.

In return, these theocrats and Sharia-advocates must accept the right of those who believe in democracy, free institutions and human equality to criticise Islam and to oppose its dissemination and the atavistic cultural norms practiced by some Muslims.

It is this right – I would even say duty – to describe, criticise and oppose a totalitarian ideology that I have tried to exercise to the best of my ability. My speech and my writings have had no other purpose than to alert my fellow citizens to the danger inherent in the Islamic concept of the state and the law.

I have made no secret of the fact that I consider this fight for our liberties to be the most important political struggle of our time. I would not be able to live with my guilty conscience if – out of fear of public condemnation and ridicule – I refrained from telling the truth as I see it. And regardless of the outcome of this trial, I intend to continue my struggle for free speech and against totalitarian concepts of any stripe.

Meanwhile, round the corner in super tolerant Holland, Geert Wilders of the Freedom Party (now one of the most popular parties the country) was being tried for insulting Islam. The case proceeded even though the prosecution did not want it to (surely a first in Western legal history). Here are some highlights from Geert's defence (Geert was thrown out of the UK before he could speak there, for posing a "threat to community harmony").

Mister President, members of the Court, I am here because of what I have said. I am here for having spoken. I have spoken, I speak and I shall continue to speak. Many have kept silent, but not Pim Fortuyn, not Theo Van Gogh, [both were murdered in Holland for criticizing Islam] and not I.

I am obliged to speak, for the Netherlands is under threat of Islam. As I have argued many times, Islam is chiefly an ideology; an ideology of hatred, of destruction, of conquest. It is my strong conviction that Islam is a threat to Western values, to freedom of speech, to the equality of men and women, of heterosexuals and homosexuals, of believers and unbelievers. All over the world we can see how freedom is fleeing from Islam.

Day by day we see our freedoms dwindle. Islam is opposed to freedom. Renowned scholars of Islam from all parts of the world agree on this. My witness experts subscribe to my view. There are more Islamic scholars whom the court did not allow me to call upon to testify. All agree with my statements, they show that I speak the truth. That truth is on trial today. We must live in the truth, said the dissidents under Communist rule, because the truth will set us free. Truth and freedom are inextricably connected. We must speak the truth because otherwise we shall lose our freedom. That is why I have spoken, why I speak and why I shall continue to speak. The statements for which I am being tried are statements which I made in my function as a politician participating in the public debate in our society.

My statements were not aimed at individuals, but at Islam and the process of Islamization. That is why the Public Prosecutor has concluded that I should be acquitted. Mister President, members of the Court, I am acting within a long tradition which I wish to honour. I am risking my life in defence of freedom in the Netherlands. Of all our achievements freedom is the most precious and the most vulnerable. I do not wish to betray my country. A politician who serves the truth hence defends the freedom of the Dutch provinces and of the Dutch people. I wish to be honest, I wish to act with honesty and that is why I wish to protect my native land against Islam. Silence is treason. That is why I have spoken, why I speak and why I shall continue to speak. Freedom and truth, I pay the price every day. Day and night I have to be protected against people who want to kill me.

I am not complaining about it; it has been my own decision to speak. However, those who threaten me and other critics of Islam are not being tried here today. I am being tried and about that I do complain. I consider this trial to be a political trial. I am being compared with the Hutu murderers in Rwanda and with Mladic. Only a few minutes ago some here have doubted my mental health. I have been called a new Hitler. I wonder whether those who call me such names will also be sued, and if not, whether the Court will also order prosecution. Probably not, and that is just as well because freedom of speech applies also to my opponents. Acquit me, for if I am convicted, you convict the freedom of opinion and expression of millions of Dutchmen. Acquit me. I do not incite to hatred. I do not incite to discrimination. But I defend the character, the identity, the culture and the freedom of the Netherlands. That is the truth. That is why I am here. That is why I speak. That is why, like Luther before the Imperial Diet at Worms, I say: "Here I stand, I can do no other." That is why I have spoken, why I speak and why I shall continue to speak. Mister President, members of the Court, though I stand here alone, my voice is the voice of many.[26]

---

[26] See also "The Australian" 24/6/2011 http://www.theaustralian.com.au/news/world/wilders-acquitted-in-hate-trial/story-e6frg6so-1226081233590

Bear in mind that these two, are the kind of people that the media invariably refers to as "hate mongers," dangerous right wing extremists, or Nazis, yet both are calling for Muslims (some of whom are actively trying to kill them) to have the protection of free speech.

Further South in Austria things are also looking bleak for housewife and counter-Jihad campaigner, Elisabeth Sabaditsch-Wolff, who ran a private seminar explaining Islam to people. A left wing group planted an observer in the audience and sent a tape to the public prosecution.

From The Gatestone Institute[27]:
The judge ruled that Sabaditsch-Wolff committed a crime by stating in her seminars about Islam that the Islamic prophet Mohammed was a paedophile (Sabaditsch-Wolff's actual words were "Mohammed had a thing for little girls.")

The judge rationalized that Mohammed's sexual contact with nine-year-old Aisha could not be considered paedophilia because Mohammed continued his marriage to Aisha until his death. According to this line of thinking, Mohammed had no exclusive desire for underage girls; he was also attracted to older females because Aisha was 18 years old when Mohammed died.

The judge ordered Sabaditsch-Wolff to pay a fine of €480 ($625) or an alternative sentence of 60 days in prison. Moreover, she was required to pay the costs of the trial. Although at first glance the fine may appear trivial -- the fine was reduced to 120 "day rates" of €4 each because Sabaditsch-Wolff is a housewife with no income -- the actual fine would have been far higher if she had had income.

In Australia, two Christian pastors, Daniel Scott and Danny Nalia, were convicted under Victorian State legislation for insulting Islam. Amazingly, the Victorian Supreme Court upheld the conviction despite accepting that nothing the two had said was untrue. Fortunately for them, they had the means to take the case to the Australian Commonwealth Supreme Court. This court ruled that telling the truth is not illegal and that the Victorian Judge had made well over 100 errors in his judgement. Although they were eventually acquitted, they suffered a five year legal nightmare and enormous costs to clear their names[28].

---

[27] http://www.gatestoneinstitute.org/2702/sabaditsch-wolff-appeal
[28] http://www.saltshakers.org.au/images/stories/attachments/Christianity_on_trial_-_Catch_the_Fire_and_the_Islamic_Council_Feb_2009.pdf

So, here are a few points from these judgements which really stand out to me.

1) People can be convicted for expressing an opinion or making a statement of fact.
2) The truth or otherwise of these statements is considered to be irrelevant.
3) Convictions depend on whether someone "feels offended or not".
4) The Government decides who has a right to feel offended.
5) So far only Muslims have been granted that right.
6) Prosecutions can go ahead even against the wishes of the prosecutors themselves.

All of these points violate the legal principles on which our society is founded. Supposedly learned and independent judges were still happy however, to pass these judgements without any outward sign of embarrassment.

Another pillar of our legal system which judges seem to be having problems understanding is the principle of the rule of law. It is the mark of a free society that everyone is seen as equal in the eyes of the law. If the Prime Minister goes through a speed camera we expect him to face the same penalty as would a street sweeper. This idea marked the transition from kings and despots, who made up the rules to suit themselves, to democratic societies which valued the freedom of all people. If the legal system were to value this tradition then we would expect to see Muslims face penalties for insulting the religions and ideas of others.

(In this picture we can just see the policeman's dayglo jacket on the far left about half the way up)

In these two photos we see British policemen, standing quietly by in a demonstration in London after the Danish cartoon affair. Apparently they were unaware that inciting people to commit mass murder has been illegal in England for some centuries, even for Muslims.

Many of these legal principles originated in England centuries ago. They have been the basis for protecting people against tyranny in fair and just societies around the world. Sadly, the UK is now leading the rush to abandon these principles. Ironically, they are doing so in order to accommodate migrants who are fleeing from tyranny in their own countries.

In 2011, English mother of two, Emma West in a foul mouthed and obviously racist rant, (which was worthy of a public order offence) told a tram full of coloured people in England, that mass immigration of black and Polish people had ruined "her" country and they should all go home [29]. A phone video of this outburst went viral on You Tube. She was immediately arrested, imprisoned and had her children taken off her. After a few weeks of holding her without charge, the Government finally decided that it isn't illegal to criticize immigration policy in public. They didn't release her however, but decided to keep her locked up "for her own safety."

This is in direct contravention of "habeas corpus", or the right to not be imprisoned without trial. It is also in direct contraventions of Article 19 of the Universal Declaration of Human Rights, which states that:

"Everyone has the right to freedom of opinion and expression; this right includes freedom to hold opinions without interference and to seek, receive and impart information and ideas through any media and regardless of frontiers".

While many people feel that those who express racist opinions deserve to be locked up, a different English judge didn't agree. Four Somali girls were brought before him, after being recorded on security camera attacking an English girl. In the seemingly unprovoked attack, which lasted for several minutes, the four girls can clearly be seen viciously punching and kicking her to the ground, (and on the ground) while screaming "white slag!" (slut) at her[30].

The girls walked free after their defence counsel argued that being Muslims, they were just not used to the effects of alcohol. Unlike the Emma West case the same year, no mention was made of "racial aggravation". After the sentencing, one of the delighted defendants tweeted "Happy happy happy! I'm so going out".

No system of justice will ever be perfect. In these two judgments however the different treatment of these women seems too extreme to be explained away by the personal preferences of individual judges. Whilst other factors may have come into play, the facts remain. One

---

[29] http://www.youtube.com/watch?v=-5RM_I6BKjE

[30] http://www.dailymail.co.uk/news/article-2070562/Muslim-girl-gang-kicked-Rhea-Page-head-yelling-kill-white-slag-FREED.html

woman was locked away for expressing an opinion. However distasteful this opinion may be, there seems little chance that she could have posed a threat to the other people involved. In fact, not one of them even filed a complaint.

The four Muslim girls on the other hand did not just pose a threat of violence. They carried out this abuse to the limit of their physical ability. They did this without any apparent provocation. Since both incidents are on film, (and I encourage you to follow the links I have provided) we can view them exactly as the judges did.

A couple of years prior to these incidents, a UK TV station aired a documentary about radical Muslims in a mosque in Birmingham[31]. This wasn't just a small mosque tucked away in a backstreet. This mosque was one of Britain's biggest. A reporter for the documentary went to the mosque regularly for a period of some months and secretly filmed the goings on in there. After attending for a while, he gained the trust of the imams and they began taking him into private assemblies. In these, preachers were spewing hatred of Kaffirs, Jews, the British people and the West in general. They were also advocating the overthrow of the UK Government. This was a capital offense until a few years ago but is apparently no longer illegal in the UK. Some of these sermons were in person and some were video cast live from Saudi Arabia.

As you would expect the police immediately took action. What you probably didn't expect, is that they didn't press charges against the mosque. Instead they tried to prosecute Channel 4 for hate speech. The police rather bizarrely claimed that Channel 4 had edited these sermons to make them seem more extreme. This claim was later thrown out by a court, which makes you wonder where the police got this idea from?

Whether these incidents are merely random occurrences, or symptoms of a society buckling under a creeping dhimmitude is hard to say. What concerns me however, is that even discussing these issues means being branded as an evil racist and Islamophobe.

---

[31] http://topdocumentaryfilms.com/dispatches-undercover-mosque

23 The End of the World

Mohammed gave his followers an account of what would happen at the end of the world. This day would not arrive until the whole world was conquered by Islam. Once this happens the remaining dhimmis will be murdered by the Muslims. The Jews will hide behind rocks and trees. The rocks and trees will then grow mouths and call out to the Muslims to kill the Jews hiding behind them. Until this day happens, Muslims believe that when they die, they will lie in the grave still awake and aware. There they stay, waiting for the Day of Judgment when they can enter Paradise.

The only ones who will ascend straight to heaven are the martyrs who die carrying out Jihad. Along with them will go their immediate family members. A Muslim mother who would normally have a large family therefore has a powerful incentive to want one of her sons to die as a martyr. This will be a passport to heaven for her, her husband and the rest of her children. The alternative (being buried alive whilst waiting for the world to be conquered) is a fairly unappealing alternative. This is why Muslims will never allow their dead to be cremated.

HADITH Sahih Bukhari [4:52:177] Narrated Abu Huraira:
Allah's Apostle said, "The Hour will not be established until you fight with the Jews, and the stone behind which a Jew will be hiding will say, "O Muslim! There is a Jew hiding behind me, so kill him."

HADITH Sahih Muslim [41:6985] Abu Huraira reported Allah's *Messenger (may peace be upon him) as saying:*
The last hour would not come unless the Muslims will fight against the Jews and the Muslims would kill them until the Jews would hide themselves behind a stone or a tree and a stone or a tree would say:

Muslim, or the servant of Allah, there is a Jew behind me; come and kill him; but the tree Gharqad would not say, for it is the tree of the Jews.

Muslims are encouraged by Islam to fight until the whole world is conquered, which will mark the end of the world. When this time arrives, all true Muslims will ascend to heaven. Those who refuse to participate in Jihad will face punishment from Allah and will be replaced by others who are more obliging.

From the Koran:

9:5 When the sacred months [by ancient Arab custom there were four months during which there was to be no violence] are passed, kill the Kaffirs wherever you find them. Take them as captives, besiege them, and lie in wait for them with every kind of ambush. If they submit to Islam, observe prayer, and pay the poor tax, then let them go their way. Allah is gracious and merciful.

9:38 Oh, believers, what possessed you that when it was said, "March forth in Allah's cause [jihad]," you cling heavily to the earth? Do you prefer the life of this world to the next? Little is the comfort of this life compared to the one that is to come. Unless you march forth, He will punish you with a grievous penalty, and He will put another in your place. You will not harm Him at all, for Allah has power over everything.

Having read this far you should by now realize that this war (Jihad) hasn't ended. Instead, it continues today in a more discreet form (in the West at least). If past Islamic history is a guide, this could be a precursor to the all-out military style Jihad, which is not yet feasible within the borders of Western nations.

24 Media influence

Previous chapters dealt with Islamic influence in Governments and Universities. In this chapter we will look at ways in which it is able to influence the Media.

Money

Rupert Murdock's News Corporation is one of the largest media companies in the world. A Saudi prince owns a 7% stake in the company worth around US$3Billion[32]. In November 2005 two Muslim youths died from electrocution whilst running from police after committing a crime. Muslims across France rioted night after night burning cars and buildings. A British newspaper reported the following[33]:

Prince Alwaleed bin Talal bin Abdul aziz Al-Saud told a conference in Dubai he had telephoned Mr Murdoch after seeing a strapline on the news channel describing the disturbances as "Muslim riots".

"I picked up the phone and called Murdoch and said that I was speaking not as a shareholder, but as a viewer of Fox. I said that these are not Muslim riots, they are riots," Campaign Middle East magazine quoted the prince as saying.

"He investigated the matter and called Fox and within half an hour it was changed from 'Muslim riots' to 'civil riots'."

Intimidation

Unless you have been living on Mars for the last few years, you probably remember the Danish cartoon affair. A Danish newspaper decided to make a (very important) point about the erosion of freedom

---

[32] Source, Wikipedia,
[33] The Guardian, 12/12/2005

of speech. In order to do so they ran a series of cartoons poking fun at Islam and Mohammed. Although the response was muted at first, an Imam, to whom the Danish had kindly granted citizenship, toured the Middle East stirring up hatred of Denmark and all things Danish. The resulting rioting, violence and economic attacks are estimated to have cost the Danish people around US$170 million. Things calmed down after a grovelling apology by the paper and the Danish government. The cartoonists have since joined the growing number of journalists needing 24/7 protection from Muslims. It is clear that before any news outlet criticizes (or even explains the truth about) Islam, they will consider the likely consequences.

Education
Journalists who cover Islam/Middle Eastern affairs are usually specialists who took Middle Eastern Studies at university. The vast majority of these departments appear to be financed by Middle Eastern petro-dollars (See Story of Mohammed Part 21).

Government
In theory we believe in a free press. In practice however, the Government will always wield a degree of influence over the press through a combination of threats, rewards and favours. You would have to expect that Islam would use its influence over Governments to apply pressure to the media. This seems especially likely for semi government broadcasting corporations such as the BBC, whose Arabic service has faced criticism for its pro Jihadi stance. Many people believe that the media is largely owned by the Jews and is heavily pro Jewish. If that were the case, you would expect to see plenty of programs or news articles which were critical of Islam.

With a degree of control over the Government, media and universities, Islam is able to spread its influence through most of the other institutions in our societies. Obvious examples would be schools (Government run with university educated teachers), police (Government run), book publishers (as with the media above) , the Judiciary (government run, university education), local councils (Muslim votes) etc. Hopefully by now you can understand why you have never heard the story of Mohammed's life and the significance it has for modern day society.

25 Women in Islam

B1,6,301 While on his way to pray, Mohammed passed a group of women and he said, "ladies, give to charities and donate money to the unfortunate, because I have witnessed that most of the people in hell are women. They asked, "why is that?" he answered, "you swear too much, and you show no gratitude to your husbands. I have never come across anyone more lacking in intelligence, or ignorant of their religion than women. A careful and intelligent man could be misled by many of you." they responded, "What exactly are we lacking in intelligence or faith?" Mohammed said, "is it not true that the testimony of one man is the equal to the testimony of two women?" after they affirmed that this was true, Mohammed said, "that illustrates that women are lacking in intelligence. Is it not also true that women may not pray nor fast during their menstrual cycle?" they said that this was also true. Mohammed then said, "That illustrates that women are lacking in their religion."

Author's Comments:

Muslims look to Mohammed, as Islam's perfect man, for guidance in all matters. This example of circular logic gives us (and Muslims) an insight into Mohammed's opinion of women. According to his religion, their testimony in court is only worth half that of a man's. They were also not allowed to pray or fast whilst menstruating. From this, Mohammed drew the conclusion that women were lacking in intelligence and in religion.

According to Sharia Law:
- Women cannot initiate divorce.
- Women receive lower inheritance than men.
- Women have less right to child custody in a divorce.

- Men may marry multiple women without being obliged to inform either the new bride, or his existing wives.

These are just a few of the conditions imposed on Muslim women. What is potentially even more harmful is Islam's obsession with (female) sexual morality. Considering Mohammed's treatment of female captives, his child bride and eleven wives, this might seem confusing to a non-Muslim.

As usual this confusion resolves itself if we consider Islam as a vehicle for (particularly tribal) conquest. As we have already seen, Islam uses women to advance itself, using their reproductive capacity to grow its numbers.

However, women are also seen as a two edged sword. Many famous rifts throughout history have been caused by jealousy over women. Helen of Troy is reputed to have had "a face which launched a thousand ships," (and ten years of warfare) whilst Mark Anthony's battles with Caesar were sparked by rivalry over Cleopatra. These are just two of the more famous examples of armies and societies torn apart by jealousy over women.

In tribal conflicts in particular, rivalries and tensions over women and particularly infidelity, have the potential to cause catastrophic rifts. These can destroy harmony and lead to defeat. Mohammed, with eleven wives and various concubines and female slaves, had more than his fair share of problems with women. Eventually these became so serious that he was advised to put them behind a veil.

By controlling women, Mohammed found his problems were reduced and he was free to concentrate on Jihad. Sharia Law reflects this, by placing women in a position of powerlessness from the time of their birth.

Sharia Law also imposes the most hideously barbaric punishments, to prevent any hint of sexual impropriety on behalf of Muslim women. These can range from public floggings, right through to being buried to the waist and stoned to death. Women are often killed by family members before such cases go to court. These extra-judicial murders are known as "honour killings" and are increasingly common in "Western" countries.

In order to prevent any of these potential "problems," some Islamic societies go a step further and carry out a procedure on girls before they reach sexual maturity. The horror of this practice (known as Female Genital Mutilation or FGM) is almost beyond comprehension.

88

26 Female Genital Mutilation

Narrated Umm Atiyyah al-Ansariyyah:
A woman used to perform circumcision in Medina. The Prophet
(peace be upon him) said to her: Do not cut severely as that is better
for a woman and more desirable for a husband. (Sunan Abu Dawud,
Book 41, Number 5251)

In another famous Hadith, Abu Musa told how Aisha related the
following to him:
The Messenger of Allah (may peace be upon him) said: When
anyone sits amidst four parts (of the woman) and the circumcised
parts touch each other a bath becomes obligatory. (Sahih Muslim,
Book 003, Number 0684)

Various hadith define legal intercourse (for purity purposes) as
occurring when the circumcised parts cross or touch each other. i.e.
Circumcision of both men and women is presupposed.[34]

From Wikipedia:
FGM is defined by the World Health Organization (WHO) as "all
procedures that involve partial or total removal of the external female
genitalia, or other injury to the female genital organs for non-medical
reasons."
FGM is typically carried out on girls from a few days old to puberty.
It may take place in a hospital, but is usually performed, without
anaesthesia, by a traditional circumciser using a knife, razor, or
scissors. According to the WHO, it is practiced in 28 countries in
western, eastern, and north-eastern Africa, in parts of the Middle
East, and within some immigrant communities in Europe, North

---

[34] (From http://www.answering-islam.org/Index/C/circumcision.html)

America, and Australasia. The WHO estimates that 100–140 million women and girls around the world have experienced the procedure, including 92 million in Africa. The practice is carried out by some communities who believe it reduces a woman's libido.

The WHO has offered four classifications of FGM. The main three are Type I, removal of the clitoral hood, almost invariably accompanied by removal of the clitoris itself (clitoridectomy); Type II, removal of the clitoris and inner labia; and Type III (infibulation), removal of all or part of the inner and outer labia, and usually the clitoris, and the fusion of the wound, leaving a small hole for the passage of urine and menstrual blood—the fused wound is opened for intercourse and childbirth. [Authors note: often, a twig is inserted into the vagina and the girls legs are tied together for around 2 weeks until the wound heals. The twig is then removed leaving a small hole]Around 85 percent of women who undergo FGM experience Types I and II, and 15 percent Type III, though Type III is the most common procedure in several countries, including Sudan, Somalia, and Djibouti, Several miscellaneous acts are categorized as Type IV. These range from a symbolic pricking or piercing of the clitoris or labia, to cauterization of the clitoris, cutting into the vagina to widen it (gishiri cutting), and introducing corrosive substances to tighten it.

Opposition to FGM focuses on human rights violations, lack of informed consent, and health risks, which include fatal hemorrhaging, epidermoid cysts, recurrent urinary and vaginal infections.

Author's Comments:

You Tube used to host some graphic videos of people performing this procedure on little girls. I had thought to include some links but was unable to do much research. I watched a part of one such video with a young girl of around my daughter's age being held down by relatives whilst the "health professional" sliced at her genitals. I only managed to watch for a few seconds before I had to turn it off. I will never forget the horror of that little girl screaming as she tried desperately to free herself. It is apparently not uncommon for these little girls to suffer broken bones as the adults try desperately to restrain them. Sometimes the struggles lead to botched cutting with serious consequences. Some victims face a lifetime of agonizing pain, even when things don't go wrong. Feel free to do your own research on this but I warn you, you will need a very strong stomach and it may change your view of humanity.

From the evidence of the hadith, it seems clear that FGM was practiced in Arabia in Mohammed's day; it was not an Islamic invention. It is also true that many Muslims today do not practice it. Fortunately for many Muslim girls, the main hadith supporting this practice does not come from one of the two "Sahih" (authentic) hadith of Bukhari or Muslim. Instead they come from the hadith of Abu Dawud. Although this is one of the four collections which are still considered reliable, there is some doubt. This is reflected in the different interpretations by the various schools of Islamic jurisprudence.

Sunni Islam accounts for 90% of Muslims and has four main groups. These are Shafi'i, Maliki, Hanbali and Hanafi. FGM is recommended by the Hanafi, it is Sunna or highly recommended by the Malikis and Hanbalis and obligatory for Shafi'is[35]. As you would expect, in countries where Shafi'i Islam is practiced, FGM is very common. Egypt and Indonesia are both Shafi'i and have a high instance of FGM. Egypt's new Islamist friendly Government is now looking at decriminalising this practice. In reality it probably won't make much difference. Around 97% of Egyptian women are circumcised, whilst Christians make up around 3% of the population.

Sadly, this practice is no longer confined to Third World or Islamic countries. A recent article in Melbourne's Herald Sun [36] reported that 600 women were treated last year for the effects of FGM, in one hospital in Melbourne (Australia). That is one hospital in one city in one year. This pattern is probably being repeated in other Western nations with Muslim populations. The article quotes health professionals, who suspect people are taking their daughters out of the country to have this procedure performed, or are even doing it in Australia.

Famous women's rights activist Germaine Greer recently weighed in on the debate. On a TV panel show she expressed the opinion that FGM is "a legitimate facet of cultural identity". She also insisted it had absolutely nothing to do with religion and implied that we shouldn't judge these people too harshly. Her reason was that Western women are mutilating themselves with tattoos and piercings[37].

This argument completely misses the point that mutilating your own body is a personal decision, but to forcibly mutilate the body of

---

[35] Reliance of the Traveller (Islam's most revered Sharia Law manual)

[36] Herald Sun 05/09/2012

[37] http://www.abc.net.au/tv/qanda/txt/s3570412.htm

another person, particularly a defenceless child, is both legally and morally wrong.

This would have to be one of the most appalling examples of Cultural Relativism ever. The fact that it comes from a women's rights activist leaves me in a state of disbelief.

When the cover up of widespread child abuse was discovered in the Catholic Church there was, quite rightly, an outpouring of anger and disgust by the whole population. Newspapers and TV news journalists fell over each other to publish details and calls for action were everywhere.

Why then this eerie silence or mealy mouthed apologies from the press and self-appointed opinion formers? Where is the outrage at this heinous crime? Why don't our politicians address it? Why is no one being prosecuted? Why don't these innocent little girls deserve our protection? These are the helpless victims of the poisonous doctrine known as Political Correctness.

27 More Suicidal Jihad

B4,52,65 A man came to the Prophet and asked, "A man fights for the spoils of war; another fights for fame; and a third fights for showing off; which of them fights in Allah's Cause?" The Prophet said, "He who fights that Allah's Word (Islam) should be superior fights in Allah's Cause."

I791 Mohammed sent an army of three thousand to Muta soon after his return from Mecca. Muta was north of Medina, near Syria. When the Muslims got there they found a large army of Byzantines. The Jihadists paused for two days of discussion. They had not been sent there to do battle with a professional army. What should they do? Many wanted to send a letter back to Mohammed and explain the new situation. If he wanted them to attack, so be it. If he wanted to send reinforcements that would be good. But one of them said, "Men, you are complaining of what you came here to do. Die as martyrs. Islam does not fight with numbers or strength but for Islam. Come on! We have only two prospects. Death or martyrdom; both are fine. Let us go forward!"

I796 The Muslims were cut to ribbons. The Christian Byzantines were professionals and superior in numbers. They were not Meccan merchants. Mohammed said that all three of the Muslim commanders went to heaven on beds of gold. But the final commander's bed turned away slightly as it approached heaven because he had paused before heading into destruction. He was not as complete a martyr. But Mohammed wept for all the dead. This was unusual as he had forbidden excessive mourning for those who died in Jihad.

Author's Comments:

Mohammed was a capable military commander. His main strategy of Jihad was not based on superior military strategy however. It was based on his ability to inspire his followers to suicidal bravery in battle. This is combined with the ability of Islam to replace these fallen warriors with new souls because of their high birth rate. With a never ending commitment to conflict, eventually Islam has triumphed in a great majority of the conflicts in which it was involved. It is worth noting that although at this time the Byzantines were infinitely more powerful than the Muslims; it was the Muslims who would soon triumph and take over most of their empire. The Jihad continued relentlessly until the Byzantine Capital Constantinople (Istanbul) fell some 700 years later.

Mohammed continued his Jihad without let up until his death, some nine years after his arrival in Medina. By this time he was the King of all Arabia, without a single enemy left standing. During these Nine years, he had been involved in an armed event on average, every Seven weeks. Before his death he sent letters to the powerful Persian and Byzantine emperors telling them to convert to Islam or suffer the consequences. They probably laughed at his arrogance. Within a few decades however, each of these empires would be conquered by the Muslims using Mohammed's tactics of Jihad. Although the methods would be refined over the years, the principles remain the same until this day:

Rules of Jihad:
1) Jihad is sanctioned by Allah. There is no higher authority, therefore it is always justified.
2) Never abide by any rules or limitations. The ends justify ANY means no matter how shocking. Jihad can be any action which advances Islam or weakens the Kaffirs, whether by a group or an individual. Even donating money to pay for someone else's Jihad is a type of Jihad itself.
3) ALWAYS play the victim. Mohammed twisted his situation around. Although he had attacked innocent people without provocation he blamed them because they had "stopped others from becoming Muslims" and had worshiped idols. The attack was their fault and the Muslims were the victims, not the Kaffirs.

4) Keep repeating this and people will eventually begin to believe it. If you can persuade the victim to accept the blame you have won, because retaliation requires a sense of injustice. If the victim accepts the blame they will turn their hatred towards themselves.
5) Inspire your followers to fanatical suicidal bravery.
6) Deceive and sow discord amongst your enemies (the Kaffirs) whenever possible in order to secure victory.
7) Never ever give up, even when you are being beaten.
8) Never ever allow criticism of Mohammed, Allah or Islam, destroy free speech.

28 A Muslim's Story

It is difficult for many in the West to understand how these events of 1400 years ago can impact the lives of millions today. For this reason, I have included an article by ex-Muslim, Dr Wafa Sultan. Every day she risks her life simply to tell us of her own experiences and the truth as she sees it. Of all the incredible things I could say about Dr Sultan, the most incredible is that she is still alive (type her name into You Tube and you will see what I mean). I believe we owe her a huge debt of gratitude for the courage which so few in The West seem to display.

The Islamists' Enablers: The Western Sell-out to Sharia Law By Wafa Sultan[38]

There is no doubt that free speech, the bedrock of democracy and civilization, is under dangerous assault in many Western countries, by a variety of leading organizations and individuals who align themselves with Muslim institutions. They all promote the fantasy of Muslim victimhood and force the West to overprotect Muslims, to ignore their atrocities and to surrender to their escalating demands.

Around the world, Muslims enforce non-Muslims compliance and deliberate air-brushing of the extent and magnitude of the Islamic threat from holy war, or Jihad, to the treatment of women under Islam. As approved by Sharia dictates, Muslims also try to forbid non-Muslims from speaking critically about Islam.

How do they accomplish this? They name anyone who engages in an honest examination of Islamic texts as a bigot, or full of hate, or call him an "Islamophobe." Dissent brings trials for non-specific "hate-speech" crimes, as well as threats of riots, violence and boycotts. In

---

[38] http://www.gatestoneinstitute.org/2135/islamists-western-sharia-law

many worst-case scenarios, Muslims kill non-Muslims, as well as those brave Muslims who dare to defy mind-control and suppression.

Only a few days ago the courageous Lars Hedegaard was found guilty of so called "hate speech" for having made allegedly racist statements. Yet, Mr Hedegaard has been telling the truth. He has been bringing to the public's attention the appalling widespread Islamic 'honour' violence, in which family members are directed to kill female relatives, reportedly to "restore family honour," for "crimes" such as being raped, often by a family member; the woman is always declared guilty, never the rapist -- as well as for alleged adultery, even if there is no proof, but just "a feeling" the judges may have as in the recent case of Hena in Bangladesh who was sentenced to 300 lashes and during the lashings died.

During my thirty-two years of living in Syria, I have witnessed first-hand, countless acts of vicious violence and cruelty. As a practicing physician in Syria, I have seen and treated countless abused women who were severely beaten and raped with the tacit approval of Sharia and family "honour."

Those victims I treated were of the same type of victims of honour violence to which Mr. Hedegaard referred, and for which he is now being penalized by those who are supposed to be championing the same values we all hold dear in the West.

By suppressing the freedom to expose atrocities and cruelty against Muslim women, however, the West undermines their status as respected and valued citizens. Is this what government leaders seek to accomplish? Are Muslim women who suffer immensely under Sharia Law, including in the West, not worthy of government protection?

As a physician, I am alarmed at the coordinated effort by Islamists and their accomplices in the West to disrupt this basic right to freely express and expose what needs to be corrected. The horrific attack on 9/11 has brought to light the recognition that no spot on Earth is immune to Islamism. My own personal stories -- my ophthalmology teacher in medical school in Syria, for example, was shot and killed in front of us because he was teaching female students -- apply to all of us.

As long as there are Muslims within our societies who promote Islamic Sharia Law and work tirelessly to apply it in our free societies, we need to be educated, vigilant and active in defending our liberties. It is one issue that all of us must be concerned about and strongly attentive to.

I am not here to incite anyone against Muslims. Please understand that Muslims are my people, and under any circumstances I wouldn't be able to peel off my own skin and be anything else but a woman from a Muslim country and the Islamic culture. But I am here to unearth the true face of Islam as a hateful and intolerant ideology, including its treatment of women.

Osama Bin Laden is now dead and gone. But the harsh and intolerable Sharia Law he so faithfully practiced is alive and thriving. Bin Laden's life and horrific actions are clear proof that Islamists are victims of an intolerable dogma that lures them away from their inherent common sense, and turns them into human beasts.

At a very early age, they are brainwashed to believe that Islam is bound to control the entire world, and that their mission on earth is to fight for the sake of this goal. For this, the end justifies the means -- therefore humiliating, torturing or killing others is a divine mission.

Lara Logan, the CBS journalist who covered the recent Egyptian revolution broke the wall of silence on a program called "60 minutes," by sharing the sexual violence that was inflicted on her as a female and a foreign journalist in the field. In her own words, she stated that the Egyptian mob who assaulted her "really enjoyed my pain and suffering. It incited them to more violence."

For many Westerners this is a vivid view into the shocking treatment and continuous harassment of native women, as well as foreign women, in Egypt.

This practice persists due to Muslim inculcation of hostility to, and derision of, women. To add salt to the wound, Muslims blame only the victim -- for supposedly falling short of Islamic restrictions on dress and behaviour and thereby "enticing" the men.

Unfortunately, in her interview, Logan submitted to the persisting political correctness, and was careful not to use the words "Muslim" or "Islam" with connection to the terrible sexual ordeal against her.

Let me share with you only few personal stories. These are tales which only affirm Lara Logan's deplorable episode, and prove the pervasiveness of the abuse of women in the Muslim world.

My own niece was forced to marry her cousin when she was eleven and he was over forty. Her marriage was valid under Islamic Sharia because the prophet Muhammad married his second wife, Aisha when she was 6 years old and he was over fifty. My niece for many years was terribly abused and did not have the right to ask for a divorce.

She would escape from her husband's house to her father's, begging him; "Please let me stay here. I promise to be your maid to the last day of my life. He is so abusive; I can't take this torture anymore." Her father would reply, "It is shame for a woman to leave her husband's home without his permission. Go back. I promise I will talk to him".

At the age of 28, my niece committed suicide by setting herself on fire; she left behind four children.

While working as a physician in Syria, I witnessed many crimes committed in my society in the name of Islam. Once, when I worked in a small village, a woman in her late thirties came to my office complaining of nausea, vomiting and back pain. An examination revealed that she was three months pregnant. As soon as I told her the news, she collapsed on the chair and began to scream, smacking her face, "I beg you doctor, I beg you to rescue me from the mess I'm in. My son will kill me. I don't care about my life. I deserve to die, but I don't want my son to dirty his hands with my blood."

"What is wrong, Fatima?" I asked.

"My husband died five years ago and left me with four children. His brother rapes me every day in exchange for feeding my children. If he knew I was pregnant he would provoke my son, who is 15, into killing me rather than be exposed to public disgrace."

I sent her to see a gynaecologist. When she came back to see me about two weeks later, she looked gaunt, haggard and ill. "I came to thank you." she said. "But they performed the operation to remove the foetus without an anaesthetic. I didn't have enough money to pay for the drugs to sedate me, so the doctor had to operate without them. The pain was unbearable. I nearly died"

As for my own story, my husband left for America a year ahead of me. When I submitted a request for passports for my children, the officer in charge refused to grant me one on the grounds that under the Islamic Sharia law I was not considered mentally fit to be the legal guardian of my children. He therefore asked me to bring a male from my husband's family who would allow us to get my children's passports.

No member of my husband's family lived in our town except one of his cousins. He was an alcoholic, and because of his ill nature, my husband had never wanted to introduce him to me. To make a long story short, I went to his house and bribed him with fifty Syrian pounds which is equal to one dollar. As I left the immigration building, I couldn't help thinking of the absurdity that we, women of the Muslim world are faced with: as a medical doctor, I wasn't fit to be the legal guardian of my children, but a drunken man could control my entire destiny.

It is obvious that the teaching of my faith did not coincide with my basic rights, and for sure did not respect me as a professional woman. Under Islamic Sharia Law, for example, male Muslims are granted full control over their female relatives. A father can marry his daughter off at any age to any man of his choice without her consent.

Tragically, these accounts that I share with you, are not isolated stories by any means. They signify tragic stories of millions of other Muslim women all over the world, including here in Europe and in North America. On a daily basis, there are countless domestic abuses of Muslim women: rapes and honour killings which are frequently ignored by the so called "progressives," who claim to be such big supporters of human rights.

Many in the establishment legally prosecute those brave people who dare to speak up and expose the dismal reality of violence against Muslim women, and the harsh reality of Sharia Law in general. Many people forbid our society from labelling the Islamic discrimination and maltreatment of women. Obviously, as we are presently witnessing, especially in Europe, the consequences for those who dare, are grave.

Accordingly, let me challenge those who are on the wrong side of history; how can a Muslim woman raise a fair-minded child when she is oppressed herself? Certainly, a male child who grows up watching his mother being treated with no respect, marginalized and abused, will almost inevitably have a distorted view that such behaviour against women is permissible and normal; and be capable of the type of cruelty that was inflicted by the mob against Lara Logan. Is that not a dilemma which affects the West's relationship with the Muslim world?

Sadly, Muslims and their enablers will keep defying those of us who dissent. We have a choice to make. We can continue to give in, or we can win people over by making it clear that our freedoms and our culture and our heritage will be protected -- no matter what it takes.

In his show "Real Time" Bill Maher, an American comedian, stated last month: "Islam is the only religion that 'kills you when you disagree with it. They claim: 'Look, we are a religion of peace...and if you disagree we shall cut off your head.'" Maher predicts that "there are very few people who will call them on it."

We are some of the very few who will call them on it. We are here with clarity and conviction to identify, to expose and we hope, to marginalize the enemies of the free world. We are here to deter the destruction of our values by those who aspire to enslave us under the harsh and intolerable shackles of Sharia Law.

When a woman living under Islamic Sharia Law immigrates to a free Western country, it can become a complete transformative path, as happened to me. Now that I am free, I do not have to allow my rights to be abused by any religious or political authority. In the United States I am a person -- equal to all others.

But how can we expect all other Muslim women in all parts of the free world to become emancipated when there are judicial institutions that help suppress their urge for freedom by punishing those who try to protect them, as happens to individuals like Lars Hedegaard, Geert Wilders, Elisabeth Sabaditsch-Wolff, Kurt Westergaard, Jesper Langballe, Ezra Levant, Rachel Ehrenfeld, Joe Kaufman and Mark Steyn among others? Too often, the West seems indifferent to its denigration by Islam. Times are difficult nowadays.

I, for one, do not take my rights for granted, and therefore I will continue to fight to protect these rights, not only for me but for all other Muslim women. As citizens of the free world, we must have the moral aptitude to fight and protect our liberty by exposing the totalitarian abuse of Islam against women.

The enemy has both unwitting and malevolent allies. We are obliged to call on those who surrender to Islam's oppressive doctrine, those who weaken all of us and unintentionally --- or some deliberately -- cause our decline.

We must realize that we are in a war. We must continue our unwavering resolve to serve as a buffer against the forces of evil. We cannot appease. We cannot compromise. We must recognize the enemies, and deter them at every pass.

We will not stifle our language. We will use the appropriate vocabulary to call things by their rightful name. We will continue to press for moral clarity, for open intellectual discourse with the precise definitions of our goals against their goals.

From now on, let us invoke the new terminology, "Truthophobes," against those who call us "Islamophobes."This is because their irrational fear of the truth is a detrimental factor for our survival as free people.

The bitter reality of Islam's Sharia doctrine should not be ignored. Real victory can take place only in the spirit of genuine inquiry, transparency, and the fearless pursuit of truth. A culture that does not respect half of its population will never thrive and prosper. Consequently, any attempt to make criticism of Islam forbidden and punishable by law is intolerable and will be strongly resisted by all people who love freedom.

When I was living in Syria, I cried often because I suffered. Now that I am free, I still cry, but for all other Muslim women over the world. I dream of a future when all Muslim women can savour a taste of my freedom. This is a dream that should be granted for all humanity and our job is to be unrelenting in pursuing that objective.

I challenge anyone responsible for the trial against Lars Hedegaard to reconsider the horrendous consequences of such preposterous allegations against him. Let us not revert to the Europe of the Middle-Ages.

Let Freedom of Speech prevail.

29 From Mohammed to the Modern Day

After Mohammed's death, half the tribes of Arabia left Islam, no doubt heaving a huge sigh of relief and went back to their old religions. Unfortunately for them, Islam did not die with Mohammed. His successor, Abu Bakr, fought them in a long and bloody campaign, known as the Apostasy Wars. Using the tactics of Jihad he forced them all once again, to submit to Islam.

Once they had reconquered Arabia, this handful of poor and uneducated desert tribesmen burst out on an unsuspecting world. In just a few decades they used Jihad to conquer most of the Byzantine Empire, (which was the remnants of the Roman Empire in the East) the Persian Empire, all of North Africa and Northern India. They also conquered Spain in the West and as far as Austria in the East. These represented the richest, most technologically and intellectually sophisticated societies on the planet at that time. The cream of the doctors, architects, scientists etc. were kept by the Muslim rulers as dhimmis. They served Islam with their knowledge and abilities.

In the early days, some of the Caliphs showed an appreciation of classical knowledge. At one point, a great many classical works were translated into Arabic, particularly by the Mutazilites who held sway in Baghdad. It has been argued that the unification of the Byzantine and Persian empires and the enforced adoption of Arabic across the area, contributed to a free flow of ideas. These factors are said to have underpinned what is known as "The Golden Age of Islam".

This theory may have some merit. It is worth noting however, that even today, Persians (modern day Iranians) don't speak Arabic, but Farsi. This viewpoint also ignores the fact that these societies were already the intellectual centres of the world. That they continued to be so for a time whilst under Islamic occupation doesn't necessarily mean we owe a debt of gratitude to Islam.

This didn't stop President Obama from making this claim in his famous Cairo Speech. In it he told his audience, "It was Islam, at places like Al-Azhar that carried the light of learning through so many centuries, paving the way for Europe's Renaissance and Enlightenment".

To understand the flaws in this line of reasoning, it is instructive to see how the Golden Age ended.

Essentially the ruling Mutazilites were overthrown by the much more dogmatic Asharites. Their reasoning was based more closely on the Islamic Doctrine of predestination, which insists that every event in the universe is directed personally by Allah. They argued that although things generally worked the same way, that this was merely habit. The classic example given was that, "Just because the king is always seen riding through the streets on a horse, doesn't mean that he might not one day walk through his kingdom."

Since Allah orders every single atom in the universe there is no reason why an apple falling off a tree tomorrow might not head up instead of down. This is the opposite of the doctrine of "cause and effect" which underpins all of today's scientific understanding.

It seems unlikely that such an idea would prevail right through to the present day without the support of Islamic Doctrine, but prevail it did. This might help explain the following facts and statistics which modern day, politically correct academics are having such a hard time understanding:

1) In the last 700 years not a single scientific invention or discovery of any significance has emerged from the entire Islamic World[39].
2) Each year, more books are translated into Spanish than have been translated into Arabic in the last 1,000 years[40].
3) Of the 1800 universities in the Islamic World, only around one sixth has a faculty member who has ever published anything[41].

Christianity and Judaism more than most other religions are based upon freedom of choice. There have of course been times, particularly when the Catholic Church was at the peak of its power, when the church worked to restrict free thought. Galileo was famously imprisoned by Pope Urban VIII for demonstrating that the Sun and

---

[39] Pervez Hoodbhoy, *The New Atlantis* 2011
[40] N. Fergany et al., *Arab Human Development Report 2002*, United Nations Development Programme[]
[41] Pervez Hoodbhoy, *The New Atlantis* 2011

Stars do not actually rotate around the earth. Despite this, the idea rapidly achieved widespread acceptance, suggesting a culture which was highly receptive to logic and reason.

In contrast, when the brilliant Spanish Muslim philosopher Averoes was banished to Morocco and had many of his books burned, his work disappeared from the Islamic world. It was only when Christian thinkers such as Thomas Aquinas rediscovered his writings, that its importance was recognized.

The freedom to think, speak, discuss and challenge orthodoxy is inherent in Christian doctrine but lacking in Islam. This (rather than any genetic superiority or military advantage) must surely have been a major factor in the explosion of scientific and technical knowledge which, from the time of the renaissance until just a few decades ago, was almost entirely a Western (Christian and Jewish) achievement.

Another problem besetting Islam was ecological degradation. North Africa was not always a desert. Both Carthage and Egypt were powerful North African empires which challenged Rome for supremacy. Empires don't flourish in deserts but in places of abundance. Egypt was the bread basket of Europe, with its fertile soil and water from the Nile. Right across the North of Africa was productive farmland.

The Arabs were not farmers, they were goat herders. When they conquered North Africa the Muslim conquerors ran goats over the farmland of the Christian dhimmis, who were powerless to stop them.[42] Silt samples from the Mediterranean Sea bed suggest a rapid loss of topsoil and corresponding desertification coinciding with this event. Circumstantial evidence backs this up with signs of a rapid depopulation which would probably be consistent with mass starvation and famine.

The overall result was long slow decline for Islam and a steady growth in the power of Christian Europe. Militarily, this was not evident for some time. Islamic armies and slave raiders played havoc for centuries, particularly around the areas bordering Islamic lands.

Despite relentless attacks however, the Europeans managed to hold the Muslims at bay. With all the richest empires now conquered and the booty spent, the Muslims were left depending on the dhimmis for income. Unfortunately for them, the Islamic system is designed to steadily force the dhimmis to convert to Islam. This left a diminishing

---

[42] Bill Warner. Why we are afraid of Islam, a 1400 year history

105

number of productive people carrying a growing mass of non-productive people.

Islam's long decline corresponded with the rise of the Europeans. They were gradually freeing themselves from the traditional dogma of the Catholic Church and building on the power of the scientific method of the ancient Greeks. Although the Muslims supposedly brought this knowledge to Europe, you would have to wonder whether it might have made the short hop from the Middle East, even without the Muslim invasions.

Between about 1000 and 1300AD the Europeans answered a plea for help from the Leaders of the Eastern Church, which was being devastated by Jihad. One of the objectives of these "Crusades," was to secure the Holy Land (Israel) for pilgrims to visit. Whilst the Crusades were hardly a great success, the fact that Kaffirs were able to reconquer and hold Muslim lands for a significant period of time, was an incredible humiliation for Muslims, who are still sore about it some 700 years later.

Attacks by the Turks on Eastern Europe posed a significant threat right up to the 1700s. Slave raids by the Barbary Pirates caused significant depopulation of coastal communities around Europe right up to the 1800s. As time marched on however and European technology advanced, Islam found itself increasingly on the defensive. More and more Muslim lands were conquered by the Europeans. The death knell for Islamic global power however, came with the invention of the machine gun.

Having a large number of fanatically suicidal soldiers gives you a competitive advantage if you are fighting with swords, bows and arrows or even slow loading, single shot rifles. Once the machine gun was introduced into conflicts however, the advantage of the cavalry or infantry charge disappears completely.

This was a lesson painfully learned by all sides in WW1, but for the Muslims, the industrialization of warfare took away the advantage of all out Jihad. They were now left powerless in a new world. This world was ruled by the nations with the most sophisticated technology and the highest levels of industrial production and scientific education.

The Turkish Ottoman Empire was dismantled at the end of WW1. It was then divided mainly between the British and French victors, who would hold onto it until around 30 years later. At the end of WW2 they divided it up and returned it to Arab control. The exception was an area of mainly reclaimed swamp and desert. This area makes up around 1% of the Middle East and has no natural resources. It was given to the Jews by the UN and is today called Israel.

30 The Muslim Brotherhood

It would be naïve to assume that the division of the Middle East was done solely to benefit the local Arabs. It is likely that the British wanted to retain a degree of control over the strategically important oilfields which they and the Americans had discovered and developed there.

Whilst the British and Americans no doubt played all sorts of dirty games in the region and propped up all manner of unsavoury regimes in order to keep the oil flowing; this happened all around the world.

Whereas in other parts of the world the trend has been for these brutal regimes to give way to democracy; in the Islamic world this hasn't happened. Islam considers democracy to be an abomination. This is because it creates man made laws which are above Allah's Law (Sharia). For this reason, any attempt to impose democracy on an Islamic country is very likely to fail. Islamic parties will simply get themselves elected and then work towards replacing democracy with Sharia (as is happening in Pakistan).

For this reason, Islamic societies tend towards either totalitarian theocratic rule (Sharia) or a dictator brutal enough to prevent this from happening. Attempts at democracy are usually either outright bloody failure (Iraq, Afghanistan and Algeria) or propped up by a secular military (Indonesia, Turkey). In the case of Malaysia, (which the British expended a great deal of money and lives to turn into a functioning democracy) a single (Muslim) party has held power since independence. This suggests that it isn't all that democratic anyway. Muslim populations will be exploding in the Western democracies over the next few decades. This is likely to create the same sort of problems there.

During the period of Western control of Islamic lands, Islam lost most of its overt political power. It survived however, mainly in its religious form. Muslims enjoyed a period of relative freedom. Women could walk unveiled, secular education became accessible to many and the compulsion for Jihad was mostly put on hold. Unfortunately for the Muslims however, a culture does not change easily in a few years, or even a few decades. Islamic societies were still burdened with many practices which severely retarded their economic progress.

The only industry which did boom was the oil industry. This was mainly run by Western companies and was unable to move elsewhere. Most of the profits from this industry which came back were lost in corruption[43].

In 1928, an Egyptian school teacher by the name of Hasan al-Banna, founded a society called the Muslim Brotherhood. This was a fundamentalist group dedicated to the reintroduction of traditional Islamic teachings (Koran and Sunnah) and law, (Sharia) to the Muslim world. It also advocated the forced imposition of Islamic rule over the whole world. They believed in the use of violence to achieve their goals. They understood however, that the West was too powerful to defeat in this way. Instead, they set about utilizing the other tactics of Jihad such as "Taquiya" or sacred deceit, corruption and infiltration.

Whilst the brotherhood has had strained and often bloody relations with many of the secular Arab dictatorships, it found a warm welcome in some of the Gulf States. A number of wealthy Arabs shared the same goals as the brotherhood. Conveniently, they also had the money to put their plans into action. One of the Brotherhoods offshoots is Al-Qaeda and you can see this structure in its organization. Wealthy Saudi, Osama Bin Laden is at the top supplying funds. Spiritual leadership meanwhile comes from his Egyptian No 2, Al Zawahiri. Organizational skills and planning, (for the 9/11 attacks at least) were provided by Egyptian Khalid Sheik Mohammed.

The brotherhood's motto is:
"Allah is our objective. The Prophet is our leader. Qur'an is our law. Jihad is our way. Dying in the way of Allah is our highest hope."

The Brotherhood has a number of violent Jihadi groups under its influence. These include Al-Qaeda and Hamas but it has many more offshoots which do not overtly support violence. The following is a list of its North American subgroups:

---

[43] http://cpi.transparency.org/cpi2011/results/#CountryResults 2011 corruption index Top 10 least corrupt countries, 9 are majority Christian. Bottom 10 most corrupt countries, 6 are majority Muslim.

- American Trust Publications
- Association of Muslim Scientists and Engineers
- Association of Muslim Social Scientists of North America
- Audio-Visual Centre
- Baitul Mal, Inc.
- Foundation for International Development
- International Institute of Islamic Thought
- Islamic Association for Palestine, parent group of CAIR (the Council on American-Islamic Relations)
- Islamic Book Service
- Islamic Centres Division
- Islamic Circle of North America
- Islamic Education Department
- Islamic Housing Cooperative
- Islamic Information Centre
- Islamic Medical Association of North America
- Islamic Society of North America (ISNA)
- ISNA Fiqh Committee
- ISNA Political Awareness Committee
- Islamic Teaching Centre
- Malaysian Islamic Study Group
- Mercy International Association
- Muslim Arab Youth Association
- Muslim Businessmen Association
- Muslim Communities Association
- Muslim Students Association
- Muslim Youth of North America
- North American Islamic Trust
- Occupied Land Fund (later known as the Holy Land Foundation for Relief and Development)
- United Association for Studies and Research

I expect this pattern is repeated in most countries of the world, especially the Western democracies. In the UK, the largest Islamic organization is the Muslim Council for Britain which is a Brotherhood organization. Since this list was published the Holy Land Foundation has been closed down. They were successfully prosecuted for funding terrorist organizations in Palestinian territories. CAIR was named as an unindicted co-conspirator.

31 The Project

The Muslim Brotherhood "Project" By: Patrick Poole[44]

One might be led to think that if international law enforcement authorities and Western intelligence agencies had discovered a twenty-year old document revealing a top-secret plan developed by the oldest Islamist organization with one of the most extensive terror networks in the world to launch a program of "cultural invasion" and eventual conquest of the West that virtually mirrors the tactics used by Islamists for more than two decades, that such news would scream from headlines published on the front pages and above the fold of the New York Times, Washington Post, London Times, Le Monde, Bild and La Repubblica.

If that's what you might think, you would be wrong. In fact, such a document was recovered in a raid by Swiss authorities in November 2001, two months after the horror of 9/11. Since that time information about this document, known in counterterrorism circles as "The Project" and discussion regarding its content has been limited to the top-secret world of Western intelligence communities. Only through the work of an intrepid Swiss journalist, Sylvain Besson of Le Temps and his book published in October 2005 in France, La conquête de l'Occident: Le projet secret des Islamistes (The Conquest of the West: The Islamists' Secret Project), has information regarding The Project finally been made public. One Western official cited by Besson has described The Project as "a totalitarian ideology of infiltration which represents, in the end, the greatest danger for European societies."

Now FrontPage readers will be the first to be able to read the complete English translation of The Project.

---

[44] FrontPageMagazine.com | Thursday, May 11, 2006

What Western intelligence authorities know about The Project begins with the raid of a luxurious villa in Campione, Switzerland on November 7, 2001. The target of the raid was Youssef Nada, director of the Al-Taqwa Bank of Lugano, who has had active association with the Muslim Brotherhood for more than 50 years and who admitted to being one of the organization's international leaders. The Muslim Brotherhood, regarded as the oldest and one of the most important Islamist movements in the world, was founded by Hasan al-Banna in 1928 and dedicated to the credo, "Allah is our objective. The Prophet is our leader. Qur'an is our law. Jihad is our way. Dying in the way of Allah is our highest hope."

The raid was conducted by Swiss law enforcement at the request of the White House in the initial crackdown on terrorist finances in the immediate aftermath of 9/11. US and Swiss investigators had been looking at Al-Taqwa's involvement in money laundering and funding a wide range of Islamic terrorist groups, including Al-Qaeda, HAMAS (the Palestinian affiliate of the Muslim Brotherhood), the Algerian GIA and the Tunisian Ennahdah.

Included in the documents seized during the raid of Nada's Swiss villa was a 14-page plan written in Arabic and dated December 1, 1982, which outlines a 12-point strategy to "establish an Islamic government on earth" – identified as The Project. According to testimony given to Swiss authorities by Nada, the unsigned document was prepared by "Islamic researchers" associated with the Muslim Brotherhood.

What makes The Project so different from the standard "Death of America! Death to Israel!" and "Establish the global caliphate!" Islamist rhetoric is that it represents a flexible, multi-phased, long-term approach to the "cultural invasion" of the West. Calling for the utilization of various tactics, ranging from immigration, infiltration, surveillance, propaganda, protest, deception, political legitimacy and terrorism, The Project has served for more than two decades as the Muslim Brotherhood "master plan". As can be seen in a number of examples throughout Europe – including the political recognition of parallel Islamist government organizations in Sweden, the recent "cartoon" Jihad in Denmark, the Parisian car-burning intifada last November and the 7/7 terrorist attacks in London – the plan outlined in The Project has been overwhelmingly successful.

Rather than focusing on terrorism as the sole method of group action, as is the case with Al-Qaeda, in perfect postmodern fashion the use of terror falls into a multiplicity of options available to progressively infiltrate, confront and eventually establish Islamic domination over the West. The following tactics and techniques are among the many recommendations made in The Project:

1) Networking and coordinating actions between likeminded Islamist organizations;
2) Avoiding open alliances with known terrorist organizations and individuals to maintain the appearance of "moderation";
3) Infiltrating and taking over existing Muslim organizations to realign them towards the Muslim Brotherhood's collective goals;
4) Using deception to mask the intended goals of Islamist actions, as long as it doesn't conflict with shari'a law;
5) Avoiding social conflicts with Westerners locally, nationally or globally, that might damage the long-term ability to expand the Islamist powerbase in the West or provoke a lash back against Muslims;
6) Establishing financial networks to fund the work of conversion of the West, including the support of full-time administrators and workers;
7) Conducting surveillance, obtaining data and establishing collection and data storage capabilities;
8) Putting into place a watchdog system for monitoring Western media to warn Muslims of "international plots fomented against them";
9) Cultivating an Islamist intellectual community, including the establishment of think-tanks and advocacy groups and publishing "academic" studies, to legitimize Islamist positions and to chronicle the history of Islamist movements;
10) Developing a comprehensive 100-year plan to advance Islamist ideology throughout the world;
11) Balancing international objectives with local flexibility;
12) Building extensive social networks of schools, hospitals and charitable organizations dedicated to Islamist ideals so that contact with the movement for Muslims in the West is constant;
13) Involving ideologically committed Muslims in democratically-elected institutions on all levels in the West, including government, NGOs, private organizations and labour unions;
14) Instrumentally using existing Western institutions until they can be converted and put into service of Islam;

15) Drafting Islamic constitutions, laws and policies for eventual implementation;
16) Avoiding conflict within the Islamist movements on all levels, including the development of processes for conflict resolution;
17) Instituting alliances with Western "progressive" organizations that share similar goals;
18) Creating autonomous "security forces" to protect Muslims in the West;
19) Inflaming violence and keeping Muslims living in the West "in a Jihad frame of mind";
20) Supporting Jihad movements across the Muslim world through preaching, propaganda, personnel, funding and technical and operational support;
21) Making the Palestinian cause a global wedge issue for Muslims;
22) Adopting the total liberation of Palestine from Israel and the creation of an Islamic state as a keystone in the plan for global Islamic domination;
23) Instigating a constant campaign to incite hatred by Muslims against Jews and rejecting any discussions of conciliation or coexistence with them;
24) Actively creating Jihad terror cells within Palestine;
25) Linking the terrorist activities in Palestine with the global terror movement;
26) Collecting sufficient funds to indefinitely perpetuate and support Jihad around the world;

In reading The Project, it should be kept in mind that it was drafted in 1982 when current tensions and terrorist activities in the Middle East were still very nascent. In many respects, The Project is extremely prescient for outlining the bulk of Islamist action, whether by "moderate" Islamist organizations or outright terror groups, over the past two decades.

At present, most of what is publicly known about The Project is the result of Sylvain Besson's investigative work, including his book and a related article published last October in the Swiss daily, Le Temps, L'islamisme à la conquête du monde (Islamism and the Conquest of the World), profiling his book, which is only available in a French-language edition. At least one Egyptian newspaper, Al-Mussawar, published the entire Arabic text of The Project last November.

In the English-language press, the attention paid to Besson's revelation of The Project has been almost non-existent. The only mention found in a mainstream media publication in the US has been as a secondary item in an article in the Weekly Standard (February 20, 2006) by Olivier Guitta, The Cartoon Jihad. The most extensive commentary on The Project has been by an American researcher and journalist living in London, Scott Burgess, who has posted his analysis of the document on his blog, The Daily Ablution. Along with his commentary, an English translation of the French text of The Project was serialized in December (Parts I, II, III, IV, V, Conclusion). The complete English translation prepared by Mr. Burgess is presented in its entirety here with his permission.

The lack of public discussion about The Project notwithstanding, the document and the plan it outlines has been the subject of considerable discussion amongst the Western intelligence agencies. One US counterterrorism official who spoke with Besson about The Project and who is cited in Guitta's Weekly Standard article, is current White House terrorism czar, Juan Zarate. Calling The Project a Muslim Brotherhood master plan for "spreading their political ideology," Zarate expressed concerns to Besson because "the Muslim Brotherhood is a group that worries us not because it deals with philosophical or ideological ideas but because it defends the use of violence against civilians."

One renowned international scholar of Islamist movements who also spoke with Besson, Reuven Paz, talked about The Project in its historical context:

The Project was part of the charter of the international organization of the Muslim Brotherhood, which was officially established on July 29, 1982. It reflects a vast plan which was revived in the 1960s, with the immigration of Brotherhood intellectuals, principally Syrian and Egyptians, into Europe.

As Paz notes, The Project was drafted by the Muslim Brotherhood as part of its rechartering process in 1982, a time that marks an upswing in its organizational expansion internationally, as well as a turning point in the alternating periods of repression and toleration by the Egyptian government. In 1952, the organization played a critical support role to the Free Officers Movement led by Gamal Abdul Nasser, which overthrew King Faruq, but quickly fell out of favor with the new revolutionary regime because of Nasser's refusal to follow the Muslim Brotherhood's call to institute an ideologically committed Islamic state. At various times since the July Revolution in

1952, the Brotherhood has regularly been banned and its leaders killed and imprisoned by Egyptian authorities.

Since it was rechartered in 1982, the Muslim Brotherhood has spread its network across the Middle East, Europe and even America.

At home in Egypt, parliamentary elections in 2005 saw the Muslim Brotherhood winning 20 percent of the available legislative seats, comprising the largest opposition party block. Its Palestinian affiliate, known to the world as HAMAS, recently gained control of the Palestinian Authority after elections secured for them 74 of 132 seats in the Palestinian Legislative Council. Its Syrian branch has historically been the largest organized group opposing the Assad regime and the organization also has affiliates in Jordan, Sudan and Iraq. In the US, the Muslim Brotherhood is primarily represented by the Muslim American Society (MAS).

Since its formation, the Muslim Brotherhood has advocated the use of terrorism as a means of advancing its agenda of global Islamic domination. But as the largest popular radical movement in the Islamic world, it has attracted many leading Islamist intellectuals. Included among this group of Muslim Brotherhood intellectuals is Youssef Qaradawi, an Egyptian-born, Qatar-based Islamist cleric.

As one of the leading Muslim Brotherhood spiritual figures and radical Islamic preachers (who has his own weekly program on Al-Jazeera), Qaradawi has been one of the leading apologists of suicide bombings in Israel and terrorism against Western interests in the Middle East. Both Sylvain Besson and Scott Burgess provide extensive comparisons between Qaradawi's publication, Priorities of the Islamic Movement in the Coming Phase, published in 1990 and The Project, which predates Qaradawi's Priorities by eight years. They note the striking similarities in the language used and the plans and methods both documents advocate. It is speculated that The Project was either used by Qaradawi as a template for his own work, or that he had a hand in its drafting in 1982. Perhaps coincidentally, Qaradawi was the fourth largest shareholder in the Al-Taqwa Bank of Lugano, the director of which, Youssef Nada, was the individual in whose possession The Project was found. Since 1999, Qaradawi has been banned from entering the US as a result of his connections to terrorist organizations and his outspoken advocacy of terrorism.

For those who have read The Project, what is most troubling is not that Islamists have developed a plan for global dominance; it has been assumed by experts that Islamist organizations and terrorist groups have been operating off an agreed-upon set of general principles, networks and methodology. What is startling is how effectively the Islamist plan for conquest outlined in The Project has been implemented by Muslims in the West for more than two decades. Equally troubling is the ideology that lies behind the plan: inciting hatred and violence against Jewish populations around the world; the deliberate co-opting and subversion of Western public and private institutions; its recommendation of a policy of deliberate escalating confrontation by Muslims living in the West against their neighbours and fellow-citizens; the acceptance of terrorism as a legitimate option for achieving their ends and the inevitable reality of Jihad against non-Muslims; and its ultimate goal of forcibly instituting the Islamic rule of the caliphate by Shari'a in the West and eventually the whole world.

If the experience over the past quarter of a century seen in Europe and the US is any indication, the "Islamic researchers" who drafted The Project more than two decades ago must be pleased to see their long-term plan to conquer the West and to see the Green flag of Islam raised over its citizens realized so rapidly, efficiently and completely. If Islamists are equally successful in the years to come, Westerners ought to enjoy their personal and political freedoms while they last.

32 Mohammed; the Final Instalment

Muslims are human beings like any other. Any of us can become a Muslim. We simply have to make the expression of faith (the Shahada) three times in Arabic. Islam however is not a human being and neither is it simply a religion. Rather, it is a system. A system which was designed by Mohammed (and to a lesser extent his early followers) to take over the world by force if necessary.

Once accomplished, all other cultures would be destroyed and replaced by an Islamic monoculture. If this assessment is only partly correct, then at the very least we should be having an informed and very serious discussion about the implications of growing Islamic power.

This idea might sound far-fetched to someone who is ignorant of Islamic Doctrine. We already know however, that firstly it is entirely consistent with Islam's goals, which are clearly set out in Islamic Doctrine. Secondly, even a casual look at Islamic influence today, shows all the results we would expect, were such a plan to be in force. Bear in mind that what is covered so far in this book, is just the tip of the iceberg.

For example, how many people have heard of a ZUS? I would guess not many. ZUS (Zones Urbaines Sensibles, or Sensitive Urban Zones) is the rather nondescript acronym given by the French Government, to an area in France which is mostly inhabited by poor (mostly Muslim) immigrants[45]. Non-Muslims go into these areas at their own risk. The police and military go into these areas reluctantly and only in force.

Many of these areas implement at least some degree of Sharia Law. In 2006, according to the French Government, there were no less than 751 of these areas and around 8% of the French population lives in these zones. ZUS's are conveniently listed on a webpage by the

---

[45] http://www.danielpipes.org/blog/2006/11/the-751-no-go-zones-of-france

French Government, complete with street maps[46]. From what we know of Muslim demographics and immigration, (and government projections confirm this) we can be sure that these zones will be growing exponentially over the next few decades.

Just think about that for a moment, 8% of the French population are living in areas which are, to some degree, under the occupation of a foreign power and it hasn't even rated a mention in the press. Clearly something very strange is going on, which isn't explained by the official "Muslims are poor victims of Western aggression" story.

Nobody knows how the future will pan out, but it looks like we are at a tipping point between two scenarios, one optimistic, one pessimistic.

In option one; Muslims will continue to increase in numbers and power throughout the Western world. Immigration and high birth rates will mean increasing political power assisted by money from the global Ummah. There will be a steady decrease in freedoms, particularly freedom of speech and religion. People who oppose this process openly will be vilified, prosecuted, threatened and even murdered. Sharia Law will steadily replace Western secular law and non-Muslims will find themselves victims to ever increasing discrimination and disenfranchisement which they will be powerless to oppose. Sporadic instances of resistance to this process would be met with rioting and random retributions. These will be followed by harsh government clampdowns on those responsible for the violence (the non-Muslims). The end game of course, is an Islamic society ruled by Sharia Law. The non-Muslims will live as dhimmis, paying poll tax to the Muslims and being humiliated.

Scarily, although it isn't politically correct to say so, much of this is playing out right now. The rest has occurred many times throughout history, so is hardly without precedent. How long this process might take is hard to know, but my best guess would be that within 30 years, our societies will be unrecognizable. Many of us will therefore be around to explain to our grandchildren, how we let this happen.

In the optimistic scenario, things will pan out very differently. People will begin to understand what Islam is really about. They will educate themselves and others and an informed debate will begin. Muslims will be expected to answer hard questions about their beliefs and no free pass will be given in the name of political correctness. Those Muslims who advocate, or engage in, violent resistance to this

---

[46] http://sig.ville.gouv.fr/Atlas/ZUS/

process will be imprisoned and/or deported. Principles such as the rule of law, equality and freedom of speech will be reasserted. All citizens will be expected to uphold them. Muslims who wish to retain their faith will be expected to understand the implications and provide cast iron assurances that it would not lead to unacceptable behaviour. My guess is that the vast majority would reject much, if not all, of the teachings of Islam and that ex-Muslims would be most vocal in calling for a total ban.

Only one of these options is possible. Which one prevails depends to a large extent on you. As one of the few people to understand this subject you now have a choice. Either you can ignore this information and wait for someone else to do something about it, (which they won't) or you can take a few simple steps to ensure that option two is the one we all get to live with. That means finishing this book, doing a little research yourself, (if you are so inclined) and then sharing this book and the knowledge you have, with as many people as possible. The best way to do this is covered in the next chapter but be aware. The world is now depending on you and those around you, to educate and motivate others. Our forefathers shed blood to give us freedom. With just a little effort we can ensure that our children do not lose theirs.

One way you can really help make a huge difference, is simply to leave a good review of this book on Amazon.com. This is very important. As you probably know many people look at the reviews before they decide to purchase a book. Please take time to do this.

A note of caution before you write a review. Please avoid being critical of Islam or Muslims. Once you have read the next chapter you will understand why. Comments along the lines of "It really opened my eyes" or "This book is fantastic" would be very helpful. I would also ask you to think hard about how many stars you leave on the review. A five star average on Amazon is like the Holy Grail to book credibility. Very few books achieve this and those that do stand out from the thousands of other books like nothing else. It only takes one review at four stars to take this down to 4.9. The difference this makes will influence the decision of thousands to buy or not, so please, think long and hard before giving less than five stars.

If you want to do more, you could find out the address of your elected representative and send this to him/her. In fact send this to anyone you think might benefit from this knowledge. Newspaper editors, judges, school principals, university lecturers etc. would all benefit (Important tip: most people much prefer to read it in print, not on the computer but contact me if you want electronic copies).

If you happen to come across an article regarding Islam just log in to the comments section. Once you have done this you could recommend people to buy this book on Amazon or other good retailers. (Major newspapers will not normally allow you to do this).

If you have borrowed this book, please consider buying a copy (or two) to pass to others. This helps in two ways. Firstly more people will get to read it. Secondly, it pushes this book up through the Amazon rankings, making it much more visible to the general public.

If you disagree with what I've written, you are in good company with around six billion souls on your side. One person who did agree with me however, was a Dutchman named Theo Van Gogh, grandson of Vincent Van Gogh's younger brother. He was brave enough to make a short film about Islam called "Submission." This film exposed some of its realities, just as this book has done.

Here is the last known photo of Theo Van Gogh, after he was shot and then brutally stabbed to death by a Muslim. You can still see the dagger sticking out of his chest.

This is just one out of a conservatively estimated 270 million people, who have been killed by Jihad in the last 1400 years[47]. In the twelve years since 9/11 there have been more than 21,000 terrorist attacks by Muslims[48]. Don't expect these attacks to end anytime soon, unless people learn the truth about Mohammed and Islam.

I'm going to leave you with a quote from Winston Churchill. For years before WW2 it was almost universally agreed that Hitler and his Nazi party were just a group of patriots who wanted restore German pride and revive its economy.

Churchill ignored popular opinion and called them out as dangerous, supremacist totalitarians. For his trouble, he was derided by all and sundry as a "warmonger" (the words "hatemonger" and "Naziphobic" hadn't been invented yet).

What few people today know is that in his younger days, Churchill was fighting against Muslims in the Sudan. At that time they were trying to annihilate the Christians in the South of the country (things haven't changed much). In his memoirs he wrote the following:

"How dreadful are the curses which Mohammedanism lays on its votaries! Besides the fanatical frenzy, which is as dangerous in a man as hydrophobia [rabies] in a dog, there is this fearful fatalistic apathy. The effects are apparent in many countries. Improvident habits, slovenly systems of agriculture, sluggish methods of commerce, and insecurity of property exist wherever the followers of the Prophet rule or live. A degraded sensualism deprives this life of its grace and refinement; the next of its dignity and sanctity.

The fact that in Mohammedan law every woman must belong to some man as his absolute property, either as a child, a wife, or a concubine, must delay the final extinction of slavery until the faith of Islam has ceased to be a great power among men. Individual Moslems may show splendid qualities - but the influence of the religion paralyses the social development of those who follow it. No stronger retrograde force exists in the world. Far from being moribund, Mohammedanism is a militant and proselytizing faith. It has already spread throughout Central Africa, raising fearless warriors at every step; and were it not that Christianity is sheltered in the strong arms of science, the science against which it had vainly struggled, the civilization of modern Europe might fall, as fell the civilization of ancient Rome."[49]

---

[47] Centre for the Study of Political Islam
[48] http://www.thereligionofpeace.com

It used to concern me that everyone seemed to disagree with what I was saying. Once I found out that Churchill was on my side, I never gave it another moment's thought.

To those of you who have read this far, thanks for taking the time. I hope you enjoyed it, I hope you understood it and I hope you will be inspired to pass this on to everyone you think will read it, while it is still possible to do so.

One last point, I constantly think of ways to improve this book. If I make any major changes, such as whole new chapters, I will post them on my blog at:

http://thestoryofmohammed.blogspot.com.au

Also posted there will be details of my next book whatever that may be. To ensure you are notified of any such details, or to hear about activities and organisations who are effective, please send an email to:

harryyo@gmail.com

(Please keep reading, there is more important information in the following chapters)

---

[49] *Sir Winston Churchill (The River War, first edition, Vol. II, pages 248-50 (London: Longmans, Green & Co., 1899)*

33 How to Explain Islam to People

"It's easier to fool people than to convince them they have been fooled" – Mark Twain

When I first learned the truth about Islam, I was shocked and wanted to explain it to people. What I wasn't prepared for, was the reaction I would encounter. My quieter friends seemed to suddenly avoid me whenever possible. The more outgoing ones berated me. They accused me of everything from racism and intolerance, to outright bigotry. This was somewhat surprising and it took me a while to figure out what was going on. In order to understand this reaction, you need to know a little about a process which is commonly referred to as brainwashing.

Brainwashing is a process by which people's thoughts and actions are manipulated by a third party. This process involves the use of a variety of different techniques, but at its core, it is a process which takes advantage of a human survival mechanism.

When we hear things from many people, constantly repeated, our brains tend to believe it is true. This is an important survival mechanism because the majority is usually right. When everyone tells you "Don't go into that cave there is a huge bear in there," it is wise to listen. That is why our brains work this way.

Religious cults take advantage of this fact and amplify its effectiveness by using techniques such as sleep deprivation and the changing of meal times etc. (many of these techniques are found in Islam, especially during Ramadan). There is however a much more common way in which this process is used by those with access to mass media.

Advertisers understand that if they constantly bombard our brains with messages such as, "our product is good" they can gradually alter our opinions. We all like to pretend that we are not susceptible to this kind of manipulation. The facts however, suggest otherwise.

Political Islam has been applying this technique very successfully. Over the last few decades we have repeatedly been told that "Islam is peaceful" and "it's just like Christianity" etc.

We have heard this message from presidents and prime ministers, we have heard it from teachers, the press, church leaders and just about everyone in authority. Consequently, most people have come to believe it is true.

There is a problem with trying to brainwash people with a lie however. Once people have seen the truth, no amount of brainwashing will convince them to believe the lie. Once people have looked into the cave and seen that there is no bear in there, it is impossible to convince them otherwise.

Clever brainwashers know this of course and so they use another cunning trick to "insulate" people from the truth. As well as brainwashing you with "the lie," they also brainwash you with another belief. This belief is that those trying to tell you the truth are "evil/dangerous/malicious" and must not be listened to. Those who do listen to them will become as bad as they are and will be cast out from society. Muslims vilify people with terms such as racist, bigot, Islamophobe, intolerant, ignorant etc. We have heard them so many times that we begin to believe them.

This process has been so effective that now, when people hear someone criticizing Islam, they instinctively believe that person to be an evil, racist and dangerous bigot. Consequently they will do anything they can to avoid listening to your arguments.

For people to come around to your point of view, they will have to admit that *they* are the ones who were wrong. Sadly, threading the proverbial camel through the eye of a needle is easier than forcing such an admission from most people.

This reaction came as a shock to me. I still find it hard to believe just how effective this process has been. Listening to otherwise intelligent and rational people refusing point blank to listen to a perfectly logical statement is an eye opener. It is as if they might become infected by it. This will probably come as a shock to you also. Once I understood this reaction however, I found ways to get around it.

This book was originally sent out as a series of emails to friends. Many wrote back criticizing me for being so intolerant and bigoted. I therefore carefully rewrote it to be as neutral as possible. I studiously avoided criticizing Islam, especially in the early sections to prevent people's brainwashed reactions kicking in. This careful approach has worked well and many people have learned the truth who would otherwise have been hostile to it.

At first glance, this approach may seem wrongheaded. After all what's the point of telling people about Islam if not to criticize it?

The advantage is however, is that once people understand Islam, you don't need to tell them it is bad. You simply let them make up their own minds. Having explained how Muslims are obliged to emulate Mohammed's behaviour, all you have to do is show them his biography. Then, even the most politically correct will understand the problem.

Whenever I want to introduce someone to the subject of Islam, I always tell them that I have "been researching Islam" or have been "reading a lot about it" and tell them how interesting it is. Most people are keen to know more about Islam as much of what they have heard doesn't seem quite right.

At this point I try to avoid getting into much discussion outside of the basics. I might tell them that Muslims must emulate Mohamed and how the Koran is so difficult to understand. Then I offer to give them some interesting material.

I always recommend this book because it is the best introduction to the subject of which I am aware. It is especially useful for convincing sceptics. It also carries the advantage of being available for free on the net at:

http://thestoryofmohammed.blogspot.com.au
Few people will read a book this long on the computer unfortunately.

There are other books, by people like Bill Warner, Daniel Scott, or Brigitte Gabriel which are superior in different ways. As an introduction to the subject however, it is the best I am aware of. By all means recommend a different book, but be sure it is not too confronting, especially in the early parts. This can be a real turn off, especially for the more politically correct.

Above all, avoid criticizing Islam until you can see that a person has come to see the truth. Even then allow them to take the lead so to speak. If people are not interested don't push it on them. Often times something will happen which will cause them to question things. Hopefully then, they will come back and ask you about it. Having planted the seed, it will often grow down the track without any further help from you.

Any time people are hostile to the truth, again don't push them too much. Leave them with suitable material and let them decide. Drop the subject and keep your friendship. Later on, it is surprising how many will come to the truth on their own. If you push them it will only strengthen their barriers. Taking this approach will save you much heartache. It will also make you far more effective in spreading awareness of the dangers of Islamic expansion.

Glossary of Islamic Terms

Abrogation: The cancelling out of earlier Koranic verses by later ones.

Abu Sufyan: Leader of the Quraysh, Mohammed's main rival in Mecca.

Abu Talib: Mohammed's uncle who raised him as a child.

Aisha: Mohammed's youngest and favourite wife.

Al-Tabari: One of Mohammed's biographers, a former student of Ibn Ishaq on whose work his writing is based.

Ansar: See "Helpers"

Badr: Location of the Muslims first major battle with the Quraysh.

Banu Qaynuqa: The first of three tribes of Jews living in Medina

Blood money: Money paid by tribes as compensation when they have killed a member of another tribe.

Bukhari: Compiler of one of the two most revered collections of Hadith.

Byzantines: The remnants of the Roman Empire in the East. At that time it was still one of the most powerful and technologically advanced on the planet.

Coitus Interruptus: Actually a Latin term, referring to a form of contraception which relies on withdrawing the penis from the vagina before ejaculation.

Dar al Harb: Literally the land of war. Refers to any land which is not under Sharia Law.

Dar al Islam: Any land which is ruled by Islam and is under Sharia Law.

Dhimmis: Non-Muslims who submit to Islam and agree to be ruled by Sharia Law.

Dualism: Most religions have a single set of ethics which apply to all people. Islam has two sets of ethics, one for Muslims and one for Non-Muslims. This is referred as dualism.

Emigrants: The Meccan Muslims who fled to Medina with Mohammed.

Ghatafans: A tribe of Arabs who opposed Mohammed.

Hadith: A collection of stories about Mohammed and his traditions. Of the many collections of such stories, two are considered without equal (Bukhari and Muslim) four more are considered to be reliable and the rest are considered to be very weak.

Halal: Literally "permitted". Most Westerners associate this with food however it really means anything which is permitted by Islam.

Haram: Opposite of Halal. Literally "forbidden".

Helpers (also known as "Ansar"): The Medinan Muslims who welcomed Mohammed to live with them after his flight from Mecca.

Hudna: A temporary state of peace with a group of non-Muslims.

Hypocrite: Someone who pretends to be a Muslim but is not a true believer.

Ibn Ishaq: Mohammed's first and most celebrated biographer. No original manuscript of his book, Sirat Rasul Allah (the story of the prophet of Allah or "The Sira") exists. What we have was put together by two of his students, Ibn Hashim and Al Tabari from their notes after his death.

Jihad: Literally "to struggle" although in rare instances this referred to a spiritual struggle to improve oneself, in Islamic Doctrine, it usually meant "fighting in Allah's Cause".

Jizya: Tax levied upon Dhimmis who have submitted to Islamic domination.

Kabah: A pagan Arab shrine which was taken by Mohammed to be Islam's holiest site after the conquest of Mecca

Kaffir: A Non-Muslim, literally "a concealer" who denies Allah's message despite knowing the truth.

Khadija: Mohammed's first wife and the first Muslim convert.

Khaybar: A wealthy Jewish town plundered by Mohammed, largely for treasure.

Mecca: Mohammed's birthplace in Arabia and still home to the Kabah.

Medina: Town to the North of Mecca where Mohammed made his home after fleeing from Mecca.

Muslim: Literally "one who submits" (i.e. to Islam). Abu Muslim was the name of the man who compiled one of the most revered collections of hadith.

People of the Book: Refers to Christians and Jews who, unlike the Pagan Arabs, had a written holy book.

Predestination: The belief that everything is preordained and people therefore have no choice in their lives, these choices already having been chosen by God (Allah)

Quraysh: Mohammed's tribe in Mecca. They became his enemies after rejecting his teaching.

Ramadan: Islam's holy month. During this time, Muslims must not eat or drink from sunrise to sunset.

Shahid: A martyr who dies whilst fighting in "Allah's Cause" (Jihad)

Sharia: Islamic Law. Based on the teachings and example of Mohammed as articulated in the Koran and in his biographies (Sira and Hadith). The most celebrated manual is al-Misri's "The Reliance of the Traveler"

Sira: Sirat Rasul Allah or "The Story of the Prophet of Allah" by Ibn Ishaq is Mohammed's oldest and most revered biography. The original manuscript was lost but was reconstructed by two of his students from their notes.

Sunnah: this refers to the example of Mohammed as found in the Sira and Hadith. Whatever Mohammed did or said is "Sunnah" and the perfect example for Muslims to follow.

Taquiya: Also referred to as "sacred deceit". Essentially it means deceiving people to advance Islam.

The Golden Rule: Do unto others as you would have them do unto you.

Torah: The Jewish Bible, essentially what Christians call the Old Testament

Uhud: Islam's second battle with the Quraysh which the Muslims lost.

Ummah: Muslims consider themselves to belong to a nation which they refer to as "The Ummah".

More Information

Why we are afraid of Islam
By Bill Warner (You tube clip)

Wafa Sultan vs Sheik Omar Bakri
(You tube clip)

Robert Spencer interviews Nicolai Sennels
(Google it)

Memri TV
http://www.memritv.org

Gatestone institute
http://www.gatestoneinstitute.org

Annaqed (English version)
http://www.annaqed.com/en/default.aspx

Answering Muslims
http://www.answeringmuslims.com

Books

Because they Hate
by Brigitte Gabriel

Mohammed and the unbelievers
by Bill Warner

Sharia Law for non-Muslims
by Bill Warner

The Third Choice
by Mark Durie

Infidel
by Ayaan Hirsi Ali

Windows into the Koran
by Daniel Scott.
Ibrahim Ministries International.

BLOGS

(A Word of Warning)

The following list contains some of the more radical internet blogs devoted to (mainly contemporary) Islamic issues. I include these because they cover issues which are often either ignored or glossed over by the mainstream press. These blogsites are largely uncensored and contain a wide range of opinions. These extend from the reasonably conservative to what might be described as a "lunatic fringe".

Whilst I believe in the right of all people to express opinions, some of these opinions are both morally repugnant and deeply unhelpful. Although it is important for societies to protect their citizens, this battle is currently ideological not physical.

It has always been my intent in writing this book to convey to the reader the difference between Islam and Muslims and to explain that Muslims are the victims of Islam who deserve compassion and assistance to gain freedom from what I consider to be mental prison.

I believe this should stand as a blueprint for dealing with Islam. We should never be afraid to call it out for what it is. At the same time however, we need to see and understand that Muslims are victims, not of Western imperialism, but of Islam itself.

Right now, Islam's most successful strategy is to brand its critics as hateful, intolerant, ignorant and potentially violent and dangerous. Reading through "counter jihad" blogs, you will inevitably encounter people who are poster children for this stereotype. It is my hope that having read this far, you will understand and be able to articulate to these people that such views are not only morally wrong, but tactically stupid.

Bare Naked Islam	http://www.barenakedislam.com
Ali Sina	http://www.faithfreedom.org
1389	http://1389blog.com

Organisations

Australia

Please check my blog for the latest information on organisations

http://thestoryofmohammed.blogspot.com.au/2013/09/glossary-of-islamic-terms.html

Australia Wake Up

We are an organisation of reasoning temperate individuals who uphold the Judeo-Christian and Humanist heritage of Western values upon which Australia's parliamentary democracy is founded.

We stand for freedom of speech, freedom of worship, freedom of expression, freedom of enquiry, economic freedom, personal responsibility, the rule of one law for all and universal human rights.

We oppose threats to our freedoms, heritage and national sovereignty and regard Islam as completely incompatible with Australian values, Australian laws and the norms of a civilised society.

Please contact us at Australia Wake Up.com

Oz United

Also opposing the Islamisation of Australia along with other issues of cultural decay contact Peter Forde, email: ozunited@iinet.net.au

USA

The largest and most effective organisation by far is Brigitte Gabriel's "Act for America"

Contact: actforamerica@donationnet.net

Appendix: Why I Wrote This Book

The most surprising thing about writing this book was the number of people who seem afraid to read it. They commonly believe that I must have a sinister agenda. Not only strangers but even some friends now view me with deep suspicion. If you fall into this category then please, at least read this section before writing me off.

There seem to be three main beliefs which cause some people to stop reading:

1) I am a racist who hates coloured people and especially Arabs. I have written this book to demonize their religion.
2) I am Jewish, or working for Jews to promote a Jewish agenda.
3) I have written this book to brainwash people into a whole new and dangerous set of beliefs which will lead to violence and oppression against Muslims.

Very few people who have finished the book still hold these views. Some have given useful criticism which has helped me to improve it. It is very frustrating however to hear "well, I haven't read it, but I still don't agree with it".

For this reason I will try to answer some of these points in the hope that people will read this book with an open mind and draw their own conclusions from it.

So starting with the first point, Islam is not a race of people. Neither is it mainly practiced by a single race of people as could be argued for Judaism or Hinduism. Islam is a belief system, an ethical code and a set of ideas which guide its followers whatever their ethnic background may be. At no point does "race" enter this discussion. There are many "white" Muslims from Western countries who have converted to this faith. Islam is the same for these people as it is for an Arab or African follower.

The reason I became interested in this subject was through a friend at work who was an Arab. He was finding out about Islam through an Arabic internet site called Annaqed[50], which means "critic" in that language. Fortunately the site had an English section and I began to

---

[50] http://www.annaqed.com/en/default.aspx

learn things about Islam which I hadn't heard anywhere else. This led me to books and websites which gave me an understanding of the principles of Islam. I have tried to clearly explain these principles in this book.

One Islamic scholar who has not only assisted me in writing this book, but has become a close personal friend, is Pakistani professor Daniel Scott. Like him, I strongly believe that the people who have the most to gain from an honest and frank appraisal of the Islamic religion are Muslims themselves. After reading this book I hope you will agree.

Secondly, I'm not Jewish and neither am I working for Jews (or anyone else for that matter). Whether or not Jews run the world, or are trying to take over the world is not discussed in this book in any way shape or form. This book is primarily about Mohammed and Islam. Yes, Jews feature in this book, because they featured prominently in parts of Mohammed's life. Trying to tell his story without mentioning Jews, would be like telling Jesus' story without mentioning Jews.

Understanding this subject will give insights into the relations between Jews and Muslims. How you incorporate this information into your own world view however, is entirely for you to decide.

As to whether this book is propaganda intended to brainwash people, consider what is written in it. This book contains facts about Mohammed's life and the Islamic religion. These facts are easily checkable and I have tried wherever possible to make it easy for the reader to do their own research. A quick internet search or a trip to an Islamic bookshop is all that is needed to verify what is written here.

Interwoven with these facts is my own interpretation of what is meant by them. Whilst any opinion contains bias, I have tried as far as possible to keep things simple and logical. By doing so, I hope to encourage readers to think about the subject and question it from their own perspective. I acknowledge that there is a huge range of opinion amongst both Muslims and non-Muslims about the meaning of Islam. What I have tried to set down are the broad principles. These are widely agreed upon by most mainstream Islamic scholars.

Please feel free to disagree with my opinions. Starting a well-informed discussion about Islam is more important to me than being proved right. Although some people have disagreed with my assessment of this subject, no one has yet successfully explained where I might have gone wrong. If you can figure it out, please let me know.

(harryyo@gmail.com)

Made in the USA
San Bernardino, CA
29 January 2016